Christian Lesher

Nineteenth-Century Brethren in Christ Bishop

Christian Lesher

Nineteenth-Century Brethren in Christ Bishop

By Martin H. Schrag

Published by the

Brethren in Christ Historical Society

Library of Congress Control Number: 2002117787

Contents

Introduction

This book is the result of several decades of research and writing by Martin Schrag. The first chapter appeared in the journal *Brethren in Christ History and Life* (April 1995). The remaining chapters have remained unpublished until now; in fact, Martin was still putting finishing touches on them until shortly before his death in July 2002. As editor of the journal, I received his approval of my editing of the published first chapter, but he did not live to correct or modify my editing of the remaining chapters. Martin's original manuscript of these sections is with his papers in the Brethren in Christ Historical Library and Archives at Messiah College.

Martin was a colleague of mine for many years on the faculty of Messiah College. He was a dedicated and inspiring teacher. He was also one of the best researchers that I have known. When he became interested in a subject, as he did in Christian Lesher, he did not rest until he had turned every metaphorical stone. That he should spend several decades on what to most people was an obscure name from the nineteenth century was entirely typical of Martin. In so doing he produced one of the best studies we have of the Brethren in Christ Church in the nineteenth century.

The publication of this book was made financially possible by the gifts of a number of Christian Lesher's descendants, and by colleagues, students, and friends of Martin Schrag. Their names are published on the last page of this book. We owe to these people an inestimable amount of thanks for their thoughtfulness and generosity.

E. Morris Sider
Editor

The Life and Times of Christian Lesher

Those who have worked with the primary sources from the first century of Brethren in Christ history (to 1880) know that the material is very limited. The writings and letters of Christian Lesher (1775-1856), a bishop in Franklin County, Pennsylvania, constitute a larger volume of documents than all the other surviving documents from his period combined. One of the values in reviewing his relatively voluminous writings is that through them we have an excellent insight into the thought of an early Brethren in Christ leader, as well as into the life of his group and the context in which its members lived.

Lesher's European Roots

The great majority of the Germans who came to Pennsylvania (including Swiss who were German in culture) did so in the first half of the eighteenth century.[1] Among the estimated 100,000 who had arrived by the American Revolution was a group of fifty-three families with 166 dependents[2] who sailed from Rotterdam in "ye Ship James Goodwill, David Crockatt Master [Captain]," and landed in Philadelphia on September 27, 1727.[3]

Three of the dependents were a sixteen-year-old orphan named Heinrich (Henry) Lesher, the grandfather-to-be of Christian Lesher, and two of his sisters. Henry's guardian and probable uncle was Hans Hege.[4] Related to the Heges and Leshers was Hans Lehman, whose sister Marie Hans Hege married; in turn Lehman married Hege's sister Anna. There is some but not conclusive evidence indicating that Henry Lesher's mother was another sister of Hege's—Elizabeth (or Barbara)—and that in 1710 she married Joseph Lichti whose last name in the shifts of spelling that took place in these years could have become Lesher.[5] Hege, being guardian of Henry Lesher, would naturally flow from this uncle-nephew relationship. The Heges, Lehmans, and Leshers were Mennonites, as were seven other families with Mennonite names who made the trip on the same boat.[6]

According to the oldest available source, written in 1859, Hans Hege "emigrated from Switzerland in Europe, in Schauffhausen, near Zweibrucken, at Ebertsen Hoff to the American Colonies."[7] The same source tells of the Lehmans, Leshers, and Heges coming together as three neighboring families. The source, however, is not entirely clear on this point because some of the locations are difficult to identify. There is insufficient information given to follow the route in detail, and it is not known at what point the three families became neighbors. A European genealogist characterized the statement as "enigmatic . . . because it is full of contradictions."[8] That judgment is too severe, but a loss of precision in the statement occurred as the information was passed down from one generation to another from 1727 to 1859.

However, the sequence of place names is true to history in that many Swiss-German Mennonites followed the route of emigration from Switzerland to the Palatinate and other principalities such as Zweibrucken, all located in the west-southwest part of what today is Germany. After living in these parts for a time they sailed to America.[9] While some Swiss Mennonites moved directly to America (such as the Ulrich Engel family),[10] the attention given to Zweibrucken and Ebersten Hoff in the 1859 statement indicates that the Heges, Lehmans, and Leshers settled for an unknown number of years in southwestern Germany.

The starting point of the emigration—Switzerland—is not in doubt because the surnames of Hege, Lehman, and Lesher are Swiss in origin. Moreover, the three names are found among the Swiss Anabaptists of the sixteenth and seventeenth centuries. The Heges and Leshers have been traced back to the Aargau Canton and the Lehman name is rooted in the Berne Canton (see p. 3a).[11] Substantiating data is contained in a study of Anabaptist-Mennonite surnames used in Switzerland in the years 1525 to 1799. The following names are included: Haggi, Haigy, Hagi, Hegi and Haggy; Leeman, Lehmann, Lehner, Lehnerr, and Leman; Lasture, Leuchter, Latscho, Lochman, Lotscher, Luscher, and Luthi. One German genealogist states that two hundred variations of the Lesher name is possible. The listed names not only reinforce the Anabaptist-Mennonite roots of the three families, they also show the great variety in the spelling of names.[12]

With Schaffhausen mentioned immediately after Switzerland in the 1859 migration statement, that canton appears to be on the migration route taken by those persons listed in the statement. However, the *Mennonite Encyclopedia* indicates that the last Anabaptist churches in the canton dissolved soon after the 1590s, the implication being that no Anabaptist-Mennonites lived there during the seventeenth and eighteenth centuries.[13] The present archivist of Schaffhausen, Dr. Hans Lieb, lends support to this implication by stating that no record exists of Heges or Leshers having lived in the canton in the eighteenth century; furthermore, there are no places named Zwiebrucken or Ebersten Hoff in the canton. He considers that Schaffhausen is the town of that name in the Saarland province of Germany, and points out that some thirty miles east of Schaffhausen in Germany is the town of Zwiebrucken.[14] The near proximity of the two towns is in keeping with the migration statement wording, "in Schauffhausen near Zweibrucken."[15] At the same time, however, there is no evidence of Mennonites living in Saarland in the time under consideration because the Roman Catholic rulers of the area were not allowing Mennonites to settle on their land.[16]

Although this seems to preclude the Swiss canton of Schaffhausen as being a place on the route taken to America, certain information seems to suggest that it cannot be ruled out. It is known that some persons identified as "separatists" emigrated from Schaffhausen Canton to America in the years 1737 to 1752. This information is not conclusive because the term separatist was applied not only to Mennonites but also to persons or groups who separated themselves from the state church, which could include the German Baptist Brethren, the radical Pietists, indeed any individual or group that separated themselves from the state.[17]

The most informed word on the subject undoubtedly comes from Hermann Guth, a German Mennonite historian and genealogist, who states that it was the practice of at least some Swiss Mennonites to proceed from their native canton, stay temporarily in Schaffhausen Canton, then drift down the Rhine River to or beyond Germany.

EUROPEAN ROOTS

FRANCE

France

By 1715 much of what became modern day France was unified under the king of France.

Germany

The Germanic area of Central Europe in the year 1700 was a patchwork of some three hundred sovereign principalities and territories. There were fifty-one free cities and over eighty independent districts... all of these territories were loosely organized in the Holy Roman Empire. The Palatinate and Zweibrücken (both the town and the duchy) were a part of this patchwork.

Switzerland

The three Swiss cantons mentioned in the article are
1) Schaffhausen
2) Aargau
3) Berne

JURA

Fr

NEUCHATEL

GENEVE

MAP 1

This was a way Anabaptists-Mennonites had of avoiding asking the government officials for permission to leave their home cantons.[18] Supporting such a view is a later statement of Dr. Lieb that there is no doubt that Mennonites did leave from Schaffhausen Canton for the Palatinate, but official and full documentation is lacking for the view.[19] Thus it appears that the Schaffhausen mentioned in the migration statement is the Swiss canton by that name.

The Mennonites left Switzerland because they were persecuted by both church and state, this being especially true in the cantons of Zurich and Bern. At times persecution became intense, as in 1671-1672 when over 700 Mennonites (Anabaptists) streamed from Bern to the Palatinate, and again in 1716-1717 and 1725-1727.[20] Levi Lukenbach, a well informed nineteenth-century bishop, recalled this persecution in the first Brethren in Christ account of the founding of the church, when he wrote, " . . . the ancestors of the founders of the [Brethren in Christ] Church were residents of Upper Switzerland, in Europe, and members of the Mennonite persuasion, and while living in the country they had to endure great persecution for their faith's sake. . . . Some of them were imprisoned and had their property confiscated. . . ."[21] Lukenbach tied persecution to the group of emigrants that included the Engel family (later spelled Engle), which arrived in America in 1754. The Heges, Lehmans, and Leshers also left Switzerland because of persecution.

The Mennonites fled to the Palatinate and Zweibrucken because the rulers of those lands knew the Mennonites to be good farmers who could help restore the countryside that had been devastated by the Thirty Years War (1618-1648). To encourage Mennonites to settle in their territories, the rulers granted them limited religious toleration.[22] Few of the pre-Thirty Years War Anabaptist-Mennonites remained in the Palatinate after that war, but those who did aided the newcomers.

Zweibrucken was both a duchy (600-750 square miles) and a town located within the small duchy, situated in the western and southern part of the Palatinate.[23] (The duchy, in existence for four centuries, came to an end in 1799 during the French Revolution.) As early as 1648 Swiss Mennonites were settling around the town, and by 1680 some of them had organized a congregation which later came to be known as the Ernstweiler congregation.

The names of Hege, Lehman, and Lesher have not been found among the Zweibrucken Mennonites. This is not surprising, since they would not be placed on any census list if they stayed only a short time at Zweibrucken on their way to America.[24] Moreover, the Palatinate Mennonite census lists do not include Mennonites living in the duchy of Zweibrucken, since the duchy was independent.

No evidence exists of a village named Eberstein Hoff in the duchy of Zweibrucken. Hermann Guth believes the hof (or village) in mind is Offweilerhof, located next to the town of Zweibrucken. It was locally called Oberstenhof because for a time it was owned by a Colonel Phyl. The title colonel translates into the German word *oberst*. Thus the village was named Oberstenhof or Obersthof. If this identification is correct, this was the village in which the Heges, Lehmans, and Leshers lived prior to their leaving for Pennsylvania.[25]

Although Mennonites were appreciated in the Palatinate because of their skill as farmers, they remained subject to religious discrimination. The Treaty of Westphalia (1648) recognized as legitimate the Catholic, Lutheran, and Reformed faiths but did not give Anabaptists-Mennonites legal status. This left them at the mercy of ruling authorities, who levied special taxes on Mennonites, allowed no evangelism, restricted their rights to land ownership, limited the numbers of Mennonites in the country, and refused to grant full citizenship to them.[26]

In contrast was the news of new possibilities in the "new lands." Even before Pennsylvania had been granted to William Penn, Quaker messengers, including William Penn and George Fox, were encountering the Palatinate Mennonites and securing the conversion of a number of them. Fox had been to North America and no doubt he and Mennonites of the Palatinate saw the new world as a place for refuge and new beginnings. When Penn was granted Pennsylvania in 1681 he put the vision of a "Holy Experiment" into practice by granting religious, civil and economic freedom to such persecuted groups in Europe as the Quakers, German Baptist Brethren, Mennonites, Schwenkfelders, Amish, and Moravians. The result was that Pennsylvania became a refuge for Christians who in Europe were suffering for their beliefs.[27]

Societal conditions also led Mennonites and many others to come to Pennsylvania. These included the "unhappy mix of waste at the court, mismanagement, serfdom, heavy taxation, bad weather and crop failures."[28] In addition, war continued to ravish parts of the countryside. Thus not only minorities who were discriminated against but also people of the Lutheran and Reformed faiths left the Palatinate for Pennsylvania in large numbers to become important elements in the emerging so-called Pennsylvania Dutch culture.[29]

In summary, the data examined establishes that in terms of ethnic origins, surnames, and religious commitment the roots of the Heges, Lehmans, and Leshers were in Switzerland. The relationship of these families to Schaffhausen is not fully determined, but most likely the families stayed in the canton briefly before going on to Germany. In the German Palatinate was the independent duchy of Zweibrucken which was a point of departure of Mennonites for America. Ebersten Hoff, where the three families resided before leaving for the new world, appears to have been the village of Offweilerhof, also known locally as Oberstenhof, located close to the town of Zweibrucken.

Christian Lesher's Grandparents

After declaring their loyalty to King George II of England, rejecting the authority of the pope to excommunicate princes, and agreeing that James III of Scotland had no valid claim to the throne,[30] the Heges, Lehmans and Leshers traveled to Rapho Township in Lancaster County, Pennsylvania, and settled northwest of the town of Manheim.[31]

In the 1720s and 1730s much of Lancaster County was still wilderness. Panthers and wolves roamed the uncleared land and Indians still lived in the area. Among the first Europeans to settle in what came to be Lancaster County (organized in 1729) were Mennonites who began to arrive in 1710 and who secured acreage along the Pequea Creek east and south of what came to be the city of Lancaster. The Mennonites who came in the wave of the 1730s (including the Heges, Lehmans, and Leshers) settled on land in the townships of Manheim, Warwick, and Rapho.[32] The first Europeans in Rapho Township were Scotch-Irish but they were soon replaced by Swiss-German people; by 1756 more than 110 of the 118 families in the township were of that extraction. Thus Rapho was fertile soil for the fostering of the Pennsylvania-German culture.[33]

The Heges and the Lehmans apparently settled on land before the government wanted white people in the area or had fully completed the process needed to legalize possession of land. They were known as squatters (which was true of many immigrants); they staked out their lands, as one historian says, "by marking trees along the boundary lines with a tomahawk."[34] John Hege received a patent for 149 ½ acres in 1735.[35] In the same year John Lehman (Lemon) acquired the patent for 197 acres on land adjacent to John Hege.[36] Both farms were directly adjacent (northwest) to the town of Manheim.

On December 10, 1737, a warrant was granted "unto Henry Lesher" for surveying a tract of land identified as "Leasure's Quarter" (note the freedom by which the name is spelled). Lesher applied for 150 acres but the land surveyed consisted of "one hundred and ninety-three acres and allowance of six acres [ineligible word] for roads etc." (As detailed below, the patent was not issued until 1766.) The land was located approximately three miles (northwest) measured directly crosscountry to the town of Manheim.[37]

In 1756 Henry Lesher is listed for the first time in the Rapho Township tax lists (begun in 1751, the lists have no records for 1752 through 1755). In this year he is cited as having one hundred acres, two horses, one cow, and two sheep. The land was gradually cleared—twelve acres in 1758, fifty by 1770, and seventy by 1775. The listing in 1770 shows one hundred and sixty acres, two horses, three cattle, and five sheep. In addition to being a farmer,[38] Henry Lesher was also a weaver.[39]

From his will, we learn that Henry's wife was called Mary (Maria in German).[40] Henry and Maria had eight children—John, Henry, Jacob, Casper, Christian, Maria, Barbara, and Anna. The inventories (goods owned at death) of Henry and Mary give us some insight into the life they lived. (See Appendix A for the inventories.)

It is doubtful that Henry and Mary were related to the Brethren in Christ Church in their last years (both died in 1784). The issue is complicated by the lack of precise dates for the beginning of the Brethren in Christ. Estimated dates range from 1775 to 1787.

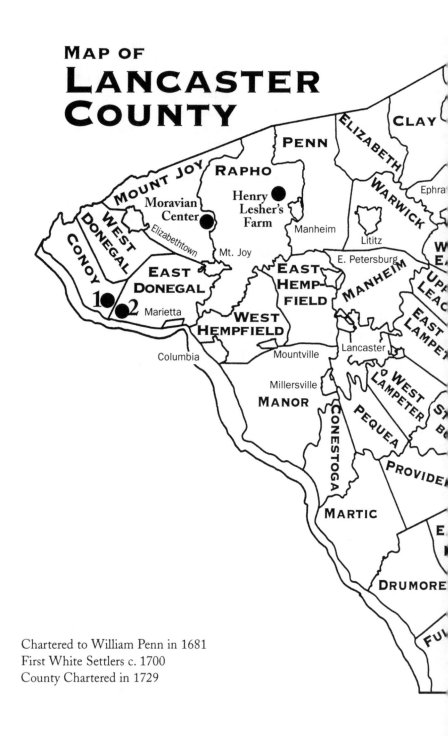

MAP OF
LANCASTER
COUNTY

CLAY

PENN

ELIZABETH

WARWICK

Ephra[t]

MOUNT JOY

RAPHO

Moravian Center

Henry Lesher's Farm

Manheim

Lititz

WEST DONEGAL

Elizabethtown

Mt. Joy

E. Petersburg

CONOY

1 2 Marietta

EAST DONEGAL

EAST HEMP-FIELD

MANHEIM

UPP LEAC

EAST LAMPE[T]

W E

Columbia

WEST HEMPFIELD

Mountville

Lancaster

Millersville

MANOR

WEST LAMPETER

ST B

PEQUEA

PROVIDE[R]

CONESTOGA

MARTIC

E

DRUMORE

FU[L]

Chartered to William Penn in 1681
First White Settlers c. 1700
County Chartered in 1729

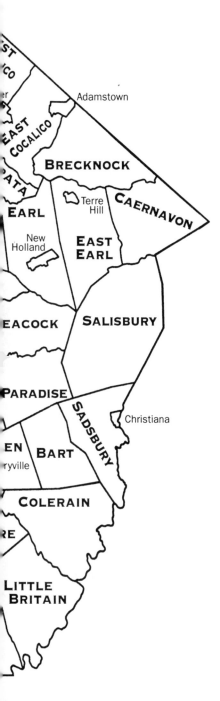

1. Henry Lesher's Farm

In 1737 a warrant was issued for the surveying of the land. Henry Sr. (1711-1784) on tax list first in 1756 (tax lists began in 1751, no records for 1752-1755). Land was surveyed again in 1761 and the patent was issued in the name of the son, Henry Lesher, Jr. (1740-1821).

2. Brethren in Christ Beginnings

The number (2) designates the homestead of the leader in the founding of the Brethren in Christ, Jacob Engle, around 1778-1780. Number (3) designates his grave.

3. Moravian Center

In the years c. 1749-1800 the Moravians had a work in the town of Donegal (today the town of Milton Grove) and carried on evangelistic work in the area. To date, no linkage has been found with the founding of the Bic, but not all sources have been studied. The Moravians kept extensive records and diaries of their work, and these texts need to be translated into English.

Notes

When Donegal township was created in 1729, it covered the present townships of West Donegal, East Donegal, Conoy, Rapho and Mt. Joy.

Henry Lesher's Farm

In 1737 a warrant was issued for the purpose of surveying the land that became Henry Leasure (Lesher) farm. The tract consisted of one hundred and ninety-three acres with allowance of six acres for road, etc. The land was surveyed again in 1761 and the patent issued (1766) in the name of the son, Henry Lesher, Jr.

John Wenger

To the right of the Lesher farm was the farm of Christian Wanger and his son, John Wenger. There is some evidence that the son, John Wenger, became the first Brethren in Christ bishop in Canada.

Manheim

The town of Manheim was/is located beyond the lower left corner of the map.

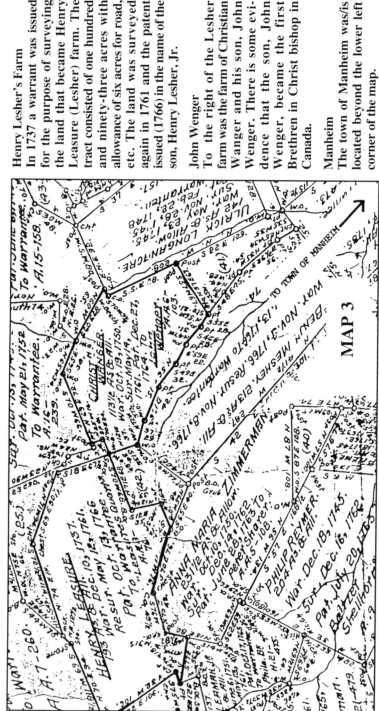

MAP 3

Undoubtedly the group met informally several years before becoming a separate entity, but the years of such meetings are not known. To the east of the Henry Lesher farm, during the life of Lesher, Sr., and Jr., was the farm of Christian Wanger (father) and John Wenger (son). Worthy of mention is that the son, John Wenger, was probably the first bishop of the Brethren in Christ in Canada (see map 8b).[41]

Henry chose as executors of his will (dated February 12, 1784) his son Christian and "my beloved friend John Heege." One of the witnesses to the will was John Hagy, Jr.[42] Probably John Heege and John Hagy, Jr., were the same person since John Heege, Sr., is thought to have died around 1765.[43]

Christian Lesher's Parents

The Leasure quarter was resurveyed in 1761 and the patent issued in the name of Henry Lesher, Jr., on October 31, 1766.[44] That the Rapho Township tax records give no evidence of the lands being turned over from the father to the son is explained by there being no tax records for the years 1759 to 1769. Before, during, and after those years, only one Henry Lesher is on the Rapho Township tax lists.[45]

Henry Lesher, Jr. (1740-1821) and Frena Zedy (Cety, Zette, 1744-1804) were married in 1765.[46] They had five children—Henry, Maria, Jacob, Fanny, and Christian. Christian became the Bishop Christian Lesher of this study. The parents of Frena—Jacob and Frena Zedy—had several children, but only Peter and Frena grew to adulthood.

How Frena (Zedy) Lesher received her inheritance is not only a part of the Lesher story, but is also a window through which to view other important aspects of the Brethren in Christ past. Father Jacob Zedy (died 1750) in his will stated that his wife was to sell the farm, pay all debts, keep the house, and live in it with her children. When the youngest child (Frena) became ten years of age, the remaining assets were to be divided equally among mother, son, and daughter.[47] Because Mother Zedy did not sell the land (she died before

November 7, 1759), the responsibility of furthering the inheritance
process fell on son Peter.

Daughter Frena was a minor at the time of her mother's death,
thus the Orphan Court of Lancaster County became involved in the
matter, and appointed John Hare, a Mennonite elder, to be her
guardian.[48] In a petition to the Orphan Court, dated November 7,
1759, Peter requested the Court to appoint several men to determine
if the land could be equally divided, and if not the men were to
determine the value of the estate so the money could be divided
between Peter and Frena. The appointed men concluded that the
land could not be equally divided "without injury and lessening the
value of the land." They evaluated the estate at 325 pounds.[49]

Mother Frena Zedy may have died before 1759, for as early as
1755 Ulrich Engel "bargained" (came to an oral agreement) with
Peter Zedy for 150 acres of Zedy land located in Donegal Township
bordering on the Susquehanna River. Before the purchase was made
final, Engel died (1756 or 1757), and because he had not made a will,
the matter came to Engel's wife Anna and her children—Catherine,
Anna, Ulrich, John, Barbara, Christina, and Jacob (Jacob became the
leader in the formation of the River Brethren, later Brethren in
Christ). The 150 acres legally became the property of the Engels on
March 26, 1761; the court determined the price at 325 pounds as
already mentioned and gave the Engel estate the deed.[50]

Frena, now the wife of Henry Lesher, Jr., received her
inheritance on June 12, 1766, in the amount of 120 pounds, 6
shillings, and 1 penny. To this was added 22 pounds and 10 shillings
for reasons that are not clear.[51]

One of the aspects of the Zedy land transactions of interest for
Brethren in Christ beginnings is the interaction of Henry Lesher, Jr.,
and his wife with the Ulrich Engel family. It is not known what all
was involved in the relationship but the contacts may have been the
means of some Leshers becoming Brethren in Christ, as may have
been the case with Christian Lesher.

Some interesting data relating to the Henry Lesher, Jr., family is
found in the records of a one-time United States federal tax levied in
anticipation of a war with England (it may not have been collected).
According to this source, the Leshers in 1798 lived in a one-story log
house twenty by twenty-two feet in size, with three windows having

twelve "lights" (the number of panes in the three windows). They also owned a barn forty-five by twenty-five feet. Their nearest neighbor was Christian Martin.[52]

It has been asserted that Henry Lesher, Jr., was a soldier in the American Revolution. The basis of the belief is that Lesher is listed in the multi-volume *Pennsylvania Archives* as a member of the Lancaster County Militia. A study of the data indicates that he took no part in the war and was what today is identified as a conscientious objector.

Evidence exists that Henry Lesher, Jr., may have spent his last years in Franklin County, Pennsylvania, probably living with his son Christian (as noted, his wife Frena died in 1804). One source states that he moved with his son Christian when the latter and his family moved to Franklin County in 1807. This statement, however, needs further documentation. Other family members living in Franklin County who may have encouraged him to move to Franklin County were his brother Jacob (1747-1813), his sister Maria (Lesher) Brubaker (1759-1838), and his two daughters, Fanny (Lesher) Wingard, and Maria (Lesher) Stoner. Henry, Jr., could have resided at more than one place in his later years. The belief that he died in Franklin County is based on his being buried in the Ringgold, Maryland, cemetery (less than a mile below the Franklin County line), beside Christian and Catherine Lesher. The headstones of the three are identical. Henry Lesher died on November 7, 1821, at eighty-one years of age.[53]

Christian and Catherine (Strite) Lesher

The future Bishop Christian Lesher, the youngest child of Henry and Frena Lesher, was born on April 26, 1775. We do not know the setting for his conversion, or when and where he became a member of the Brethren in Christ Church, although his birth corresponded to the church's beginning and he was a part of the second generation of Brethren in Christ. His being elected a bishop in 1825 meant that he knew Jacob Engel (died 1833), the first Brethren in Christ leader, and undoubtedly other first-generation leaders.[54]

Christian Lesher recorded in his Sauer Bible that he was married on August 21, 1798, to Catherine Strite (born August 21, 1779), daughter of Christian and Mary (Myers) Strite of Lancaster County (the Strite family came from the Palatinate in Germany). Six children were born to the couple—Magdalena (1801), Christian (1804), John (1810), Catherine (1815), Henry (1817), and Jacob S. (1819).[55]

Evidence indicates that Christian Lesher farmed in Rapho Township until 1806. The township tax list included a Christian Lesher as early as 1772 and a second Christian Lesher for 1800-1806, without making a distinction between the two names. The 1798 United States federal tax list noted above does make a distinction between the two names, one being designated as senior and the other as junior. It is known that the senior-junior distinction sometimes indicated an uncle-nephew relationship. Such appears to have been the case here.[56] The uncle Christian's appearance on the tax lists by 1772 relates well to his birth date; his having no sons eliminates the younger Christian as being his son.

The statistical data suggests that the younger man was the future bishop. He married in 1798 and moved to Franklin County in 1807 (see note 57 for the latter date), and was on the Rapho tax list in the years between those dates (1800-1806).[57] In short, Christian Lesher, Sr., was an uncle to the Christian Lesher of this account.[58]

Although the 1798 United States federal tax lists the two Christian Leshers as senior and junior, it does not indicate which of the two farms belonged to the uncle and which to the nephew. It appears that it was the uncle who lived in a one-story log house, twenty-eight by twenty-five feet, with three windows and eight lights. His log barn was forty-two by twenty-two feet. The name of his closest neighbor was John Isten. His nephew's log house was twenty-seven by twenty-five feet, with two windows and twelve lights; the barn was sixty by twenty-seven feet, his spring house fourteen by sixteen feet. His nearest neighbor was his father Henry.[59]

Given the nature of the sources used in this chapter, such as tax lists, patents, and deeds, most of the action is by men. Fortunately, two items were found in the Christian Lesher collection that relate to his wife Catherine. One is a piece of fraktur art featuring flowers. The writing on the left side reads "Gatarina Streitlin, Anno 1785."

Catherine Streit's fraktur

There can be little doubt that the Gatarina refers to Catherine, although in German the "G" should have been a "K." The date 1785 also suitably fits the picture since Catherine, born in 1779, would have been six years of age. Giving a student (especially young students) a piece of *fraktur* art as a reward for outstanding work was a common practice in those days, a practice commended by the well-known colonial schoolmaster, Christopher Dock.[60]

Catherine Strite's fraktur features four skillfully drawn tulips with a fan-shaped flower at the top,[61] possibly representing a carnation. The original colors were red and green.

A second item relating to Catherine Lesher is her song book. On the first page, in translation, are the following words:

> This Book of Spiritual Verses belongs to me Katherine Lesher
> purchased February 7, 1833
> Whoever intends to see the kingdom of God
> Must follow the Lamb of God in His way
> Going out with you and going out with time
> is to enter into eternal life[62] (See p. 13b)

The title of the book is *Das kleine davidische Psalterspiel der Kinder Zions* (the *Small Davidic Psalter of the Children of Zion*), first printed in 1744 by the German Baptist Brethren.[63] The song book was repeatedly republished, with minor changes from time to time. Catherine Lesher's owning a copy is evidence that at least some Brethren in Christ related to this popular book. A second piece of Fraktur art, not related to Catherine Lesher or another designated person, was found in Christian Lesher's Sauer Bible. The five stanzas of poetry carry a pietistic-oriented message that sought to edify and admonish fellow believers.[64]

Franklin County Beginnings

Europeans began settling in what became Franklin County in the 1720s. The county was organized in 1784; up to that time it had been a part of Lancaster County from 1729 to 1750 and of Cumberland County from 1750-1784.[65] Settlers purchased the land from the Indians in 1736.[66] The first settlers were Scotch-Irish who were followed shortly in larger numbers by German-speaking pioneers. When the Revolutionary War ended the threat of Indian attack, many more people, especially those with German background, settled in the county.[67]

As early as 1734, Presbyterians sent out clergymen to minister to the scattered settlers. Within a year or two, the first Mennonites made their appearance. Itinerant Lutheran pastors began serving Lutherans during the 1740s. At the same time, German Reformed believers made their way to the territory, in time becoming a strong body, probably in part because of such schools as the German Reformed Seminary in Mercersburg, a town located some twenty miles southwest of Chambersburg. German Baptist Brethren lived in the county for some years prior to organizing their first congregation in 1752. A few years later, in the 1790s, the Methodists and the United Brethren appeared in the county.[68]

Little is known about Brethren in Christ beginnings in Franklin County and of Washington County, Maryland. (Since the majority of the members lived in Franklin County, the entire community, including members in Maryland, were frequently defined as the Franklin County Brethren.) Two factors about their beginning in the counties are important to note. First, it is not always known when individuals and families began to identify with the Brethren in Christ Church. Some were members when they arrived; others became Brethren during their time in the two counties.[69] Second, it is not fully possible to determine how solid the research is that lies behind some of the available data.

In Franklin County, Christian Lesher became a minister (the date of his ordination is unknown). When he was chosen as the first resident bishop in 1825, he became the chief shepherd of the Brethren in Christ community. Given the Brethren understanding of community, the range of his leadership went beyond conventional personal spirituality to cover the scope of Brethren society. This group gradually grew, as suggested by the accounts of the following families who became Brethren in Christ.

Thanks to the detailed work of genealogist Richard Winger, it is known that Abraham Wingert (ca. 1765-1830) moved from Dauphin County (now Lebanon County) to Franklin County in 1790 where he bought land. He is listed as being a farmer and a minister of the Brethren in Christ.[70] Samuel Betzner, Sr., one of the eight men who signed the original (or first) Brethren in Christ statement of belief (ca. 1780), and his wife Mariah (or Mary), moved from Donegal Township in Lancaster County to Franklin County in 1793, buying land in Green Township, later (in 1795) adding land in Montgomery Township. Between March 1795 and April 16, 1796, the Betzners bought land across the Pennsylvania border in Maryland and from there moved to Ontario, Canada, in 1800.[71] Christian and Jacob Heisey are on the Washington Township, Franklin County, tax lists in 1799 and 1802; in 1803 they resettled in Guilford Township and in 1804, one or both men moved to Ontario, Canada.[72]

There is evidence that John Sollenberger and his mother Catherine (his father died in 1792) sold their farm in Chester County in 1794 and moved to Franklin County.[73] Heinrich Huber (Hoover)(1759-1833) and his wife Maria (Wenger) are reported to have bought 400 acres on land located in Letterkenny Township in 1800. Their son, Christian (1793-1867), became the founder and first leader of the Hooverites, which body very soon became the Franklin County wing of the Old Order River Brethren.[74] At about the same time, some Stricklers (of Swiss-German descent) from York County made their way to Franklin County. One source states that the first Strickler to arrive was Henry (1750-1816) who settled near Greencastle in 1807, followed soon by his brother Joseph (1764-1813). A Strickler genealogy mentions a Jacob Strickler moving from York to Franklin County.[75]

John and Barbara Meyer, after living in Lancaster County in the 1780s and 1790s and later in Cumberland County, by the end of the 1800 decade were living on land in Letterkenny Township in Franklin County. During their time in Lancaster County they may have taken part in the formation of the Brethren in Christ Church, since one of the persons who signed the original statement of beliefs was a John Meyer.[76] Possibly related to John and Barbara was Henry Meyers (1760-1836). Of German Baptist Brethren parentage, he moved with his family from Adams County, Pennsylvania, to Washington Township in Franklin County by 1825. He is known to have been a member and a minister of the Brethren in Christ Church, but the date of his joining the church or of his election to the ministry are not known.[77]

In 1827 Christian Oberholser, Jr. (1803-1872) (first wife Nancy Hoover, second wife Veronica Heisey) purchased a farm in Green Township, Franklin County.[78] His son was Martin H. Oberholser, a gifted future bishop.[79] Also providing leadership for the Brethren group was the Joseph Zook family (first wife Anna Schock, second wife Catherine Whisler). They lived in Lancaster County until 1829 or 1830; in the latter year, they bought a farm in Franklin County.[80] Two of their sons were elected to the Brethren in Christ ministry—Samuel, who was bishop in Franklin County and later in Dickinson County (Kansas), and Noah, pioneer Brethren evangelist, holiness preacher, church planter, and minister in the same locations his brother served as bishop.[81]

The Stoner family is known to have bought land in Washington County, Maryland (near Ringgold) by 1744. No information is available, however, concerning the family's early religious commitment, but it is known that some descendants became Brethren in Christ, including Martin (b. 1796), his brother Benjamin (b. 1806), and the latter's son Jacob (b. 1848). Martin apparently became a minister. But the dates of their becoming Brethren in Christ and of Martin's becoming a minister are not known.[82]

Another family that related to the Brethren in Christ was the Hollinger family who settled in Franklin County in 1797. More data is needed to determine which members of the family joined the Brethren, but it is known that Daniel Hollinger (1827-1895) did so; eventually he served as a deacon, as did his son-in-law D. Frank Kipe (1865-1933) for many years in the Ringgold District.[83]

In 1806 the Dayhoff family settled in Washington County, Maryland. Although members of the United Brethren Church, a son Samuel (1799-1877) joined the Brethren in Christ, as did his son John. Samuel served many years as a deacon. Both men were mechanically talented—the father in working with wood, his son in developing "mechanical devices."[84]

Members of the Deardorff family were living in Franklin County by 1802 as part of the German Baptist Brethren community. The immigrant father, Anthony, had come to Pennsylvania in either 1719 or 1729. Deardorffs have joined the Brethren in Christ in more recent years.[85]

The family of Daniel Jacobs (1787-1838) also associated with the Brethren in Christ. Coming from Adams County, Pennsylvania, to Washington County, Maryland (in the Leitersburg area), they rented a farm that was the property of Daniel Jacob's father-in-law, Henry Meyer. Daniel's hired man, Jacob Hykes (1813-1889), married Daniel's daughter Barbara; the young couple lived on a farm that Daniel and his wife Eve bought from Eve's parents. The Brethren frequently held worship services on this farm when it was owned by the Jacobs and later by the Hykes.[86]

Not readily discernable is the time and place of the arrival of the Byers family (also spelled Boyer or Bayer) in Franklin County. Henry Bayer settled in York County, Pennsylvania, around 1720. One of his descendants, Brethren in Christ minister Benjamin Boyer (b. 1788), lived below Roxbury in Letterkenny Township, Franklin County. Since that time, the Byers family have lived in the county, including William Boyer (1826-1897), and Alfred Byers (1860-1954), the grandfather and the father, respectively, of Bishop Charlie Byers.[87]

The Hawbakers came to Pennsylvania from Switzerland by way of the Palatinate and Holland. A historical sketch of the Hawbaker lineage indicates that the family belonged to "plain sects," such as the Mennonites and German Baptists. Burial and land records suggest that the family settled in Lancaster County in 1737. Three sons of a Christian Hawbaker moved to Franklin County—John to Welsh Run in 1812, Peter to Greencastle in 1810, and Henry to Upton in 1813. According to available records, the first Hawbaker to become Brethren in Christ was John (1807-1878), son of the John Hawbaker who had settled in Welsh Run. He chose to be part of the Old Order River Brethren at the time of the division of the Brethren; he is reported to have been one of the earliest bishops of the Old Order group in Franklin County.[88]

The Bert family, of Waldensian and Huguenot background and consisting of mother Elizabeth and two sons, Peter and Jacob, arrived in Chambersburg, Pennsylvania, from Frankfurt, Germany, in 1830. Peter (1812-1880) was a weaver by trade; he obtained employment with Jacob Wenger, a fellow weaver and a Brethren in Christ. Peter lived with the Wenger family for a time; their deep religious commitment led to Peter's conversion. In time he was ordained as a Brethren in Christ minister and had a wide reputation for fruitful and effective service. His daughter Sarah gave strong leadership to the founding and, for many years, the operation of the Brethren in Christ mission in Chicago.[89]

No doubt additional research would reveal other families who made their way to Franklin County and who were either Brethren in Christ before going or became so after their arrival. The data collected indicates that many of those who related to the Brethren in Christ were of Swiss-German extraction, and had earlier lived in Lancaster or the surrounding counties. There is no record of Brethren in Christ moving to Franklin County in a group; rather the pattern was more by individual families. More important for this article is that those who moved to Franklin County were a part of the group led by Christian Lesher and other church leaders.

Little is known about church life among the Brethren in Christ living in Franklin County during the years Christian Lesher was a minister and bishop. Asa W. Climenhaga, writing in the early 1940s, noted that Christian Lesher was elected bishop in 1825, and that he was assisted in the ministry by Henry Funk and Joseph Wingert (the latter was elected to the ministry in 1845 and to the bishopric in 1857).[90] Laban Brechbill, an Old Order River Brethren historian, has written that Christian (Huber) Hoover was chosen as bishop in 1834 and that Christian Oberholser also became bishop at about the same time.[91]

Precisely when the Brethren in Franklin County and Washington County, Maryland, divided into two districts is not known, but as of 1846 the North Franklin County District was operative. A one-page wheel chart shows the Sunday house meetings in a sixteen-week sequence with the family heads responsible for hosting the services.[92] A similar chart in square format and dated 1852 from the Christian Lesher collection appears to show the meeting places of the South Franklin District.[93] It will be noted that in the square chart the places of meeting are given in both German and English (illustrating the shift from the use of the German language to English), and that five of the twenty-four meeting places were in school houses.

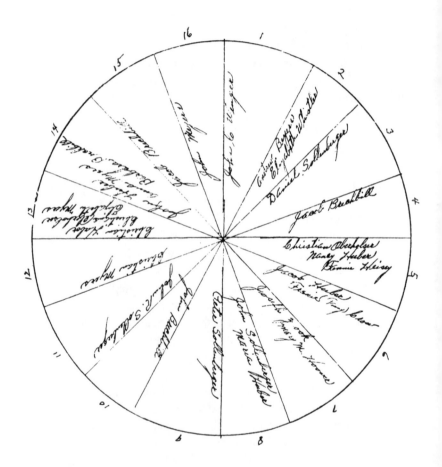

Places of Meeting of the River Brethren of the North Franklin District in 1846

The names listed in the circle chart are:

1. John C. Winger
2. Andrew Beyers
   Elizabth Whislter
3. Daniel Sollenberger
4. Jacob Breckbill
5. Christian Oberholser
   Nancy Huber
   Fannie Heisey
6. Jacob Huber
   F ? (Fanny) Crow
7. Joseph Zook
   Mary M. Hoover
8. John Sollenberger
   Maria Huber
9. Peter Sollenberger
10. John Brechbill
11. John R. Sollenberger
12. Christian Myers
13. Christiana Huber
    Christian Oberholser
    Elizabeth Myers
14. John Huber
    Anna Myers
    Barbara Brechbill
15. Jacob Brechbill
16. John Meyers

The circle chart (reduced in size) on the opposite page lists the places (homes) of Sunday house meetings in a sixteen-week sequence with the hosting families or persons for each worship service. It is not known when the River Brethren living in Franklin County (PA) and Washington County (MD) divided into the North and South Franklin Districts. The heading above suggests that as of 1846 the separation had taken place. Although it can not be stated with absolute certainty, the evidence in hand suggests that number five, Christian Oberholser, and number thirteen, Christian Huber (Hoover), were River Brethren bishops, since it is known that men with those names were bishops in Franklin County at the time. The women listed probably were the wives of the host men, but it is difficult to believe eight or nine of the men were not married. Also perplexing is the listing of more than one wife. The solution may be in keeping with the marriages of Christian Oberholser: he married Nancy Huber and after her death married Fannie Heisey.

The chart is provided through the courtesy of Jacob and Ada Sollenberger.

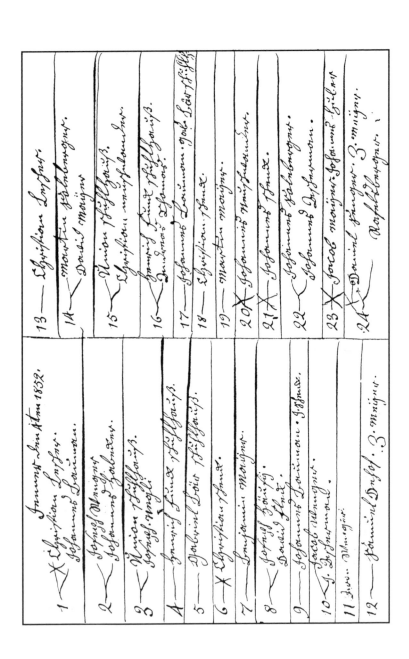

Gemeinde im Jahr 1852.

1 — Christian Luther.
Johannes Lorimer.

2 — Jakob Morgner.
Johannes Zahnmer.

3 — Union Süßholz.
Jakob Mögli.

4 — Heinrich Fürst Süßholz.

5 — Gabriel Dürst Süßholz.

6 — Christian Fürst.

7 — Benjamin Morgner.

8 — Jakob Fürst.
David Fürst.

9 — Johannes Lorimer. Johner.

10 — Jakob Morgner.

11 — J. Morgner.

12 — Heinrich Dufour. 3 Morgner.

13 — Christian Luther.

14 — Martin Zahnmer.
David Morgner.

15 — Union Süßholz.
Christian Morgner Johner.

16 — Heinrich Fürst Süßholz.
Benjamin Zahnmer.

17 — Johannes Lorimer. Jakob Lauf Fürst.

18 — Christian Fürst.

19 — Martin Morgner.

20 — Johannes Zahnmer.

21 — Johannes Fürst.

22 — Johannes Zahnmer.
Johannes Zahnmer.

23 — Jacob Morgner Johannes Gilart.

24 — David Fürst. 3 Morgner.
Raphael Morgner.

Beginning January 4th. 1852.	13 — Christian Lesher.
1 — Christian Lesher.	14 — Martin Solleberger.
John Bowman	David Myers
2 — Joseph Wenger.	15 — Union Schoolhouse.
John Hautecker.	Christian Highswander.
3 — Union Schoolhouse.	16 — Henry Frank Schoolhouse.
Joseph Fegley!	Andrew Thomas
4 — Henry Frick Schoolhouse.	17 — John Bowman.
5 — Gabriel Bear Schoolhouse.	18 — Christian Thank.
6 — Cristian Thank.	19 — Martin Myers.
7 — Benjamin Myers.	20 — John Highswander.
8 — Joseph Wysey.	21 — John Flack.
David Flack.	22 — John Solleberger.
9 — John Bowman.	John Busherman.
10 — Jacob Wenger.	23 — Jacob Myers.
John Busherman.	24 — Daniel Senger.
11	Rafelsberger.
12 — Samuel Debuf.	

Meeting places for Sunday worship sevices for the South Franklin District, 1852. The first chart is in German, the second gives the English translation. The charts were found in Christian Lesher's Sauer Bible.

The members in Franklin County in 1880 formed one of the largest sections of the Brethren in Christ Church. According to a tabulation of families made in that year, Lancaster County had 105 families, Franklin County and Washington County, Maryland, had 102, while Blair County, Pennsylvania, and York County, Ontario, each had forty-seven.[94]

Franklin County also had a good complement of ministers. A history prepared for the centennial celebration of Chambersburg held on July 4, 1876, although perhaps not deeply researched, lists four Brethren in Christ bishops and seventeen preachers. (Identified as "River Brethren," the list does not contain the names of any Old Order River Brethren.). The list reads as follows:

Bishops

Joseph Wenger	Samuel Zook
Henry Lesher	Aaron Wenger

Ministers

John Burkhart	Abraham Lesher
John Bert	Isaac Shank
Noah Zook	L. C. Wenger
Michael Wenger	George Wenger
William Tanner	John Sollenberger
Christian Stoner	Eli Martin
Jacob Lesher	Benjamin Myers [95]

The Franklin County Brethren were known as industrious people, skilled in the art of farming. A Franklin County historian in 1887 saw them as "a quiet and industrious . . . people."[96] Another writer, also having Franklin County in mind, wrote, "The sleekest and strongest horses that pull loads of grain to our elevators are those of the Mennonites, Dunkers, and River Brethren [Brethren in Christ]," and added that they had some of the best cows in the country.[97]

Of great importance, the evidence indicates that the Brethren in Christ were successful in evangelizing their friends and neighbors, although by what methods is not fully known. Avery Zook credits some of this evangelizing and consequent expansion to Christian

Lesher. He also mentions one of the ministers, Joseph M. Hess (1833-1876), as one also much interested in evangelism. Probably one of the reasons for building the Ringgold Meetinghouse in 1871 was the growth of the Brethren in Christ community in the area.[98]

Although the factual data on Brethren in Christ life in Franklin County, Pennsylvania, and Washington County, Maryland, is limited, the information gives the impression that the Brethren in Christ comprised a growing and healthy community through much of the nineteenth century.

Christian Lesher as Farmer

When Christian and Catherine Lesher moved to Franklin County in 1807, they had two children—Magdalena (age six) and Christian Jr. (age three). In the following year, the Leshers purchased 151 acres and allowances for the sum of 1,126 pounds and 10 shillings (Pennsylvania money). The farm had been given the name Dunhaven. Located in Washington Township directly north of Waynesboro, Pennsylvania, it was first surveyed in 1786 for Samuel Wilson who took possession on November 15, 1786. He sold the farm to Charles Shull on December 6, 1793, and Shull in turn sold it to the Leshers on October 4, 1808. (For the verbatim description of the initial survey, see note.)[99]

One of the neighbors to the Christian Leshers was a man named John Price. He may have been a German Baptist Brethren minister. Whether true or not, the presence of the Antietam German Baptist Brethren meeting house located one and a half miles north of Waynesboro means that the Leshers lived in an area that had a German Baptist Brethren presence. The Antietam German Baptist congregation organized themselves in 1752 and in 1795 built their meetinghouse.[100] Mennonites also lived in the area as evidenced in the Reformed Mennonite Church building situated a few miles south of Waynesboro within yards of the Franklin County, Pennsylvania, and Washington County, Maryland, border along the road from Waynesboro to Ringgold. The building was erected in the 1830s.[101]

The Leshers were involved in buying and selling land. In 1820 they bought four acres and eighty-four perches from James Coughran

The map is from *Atlas of Franklin County* printed in 1868 by Pomeroy and Beers, Chicago, and reprinted in 1974 by the Bookmark Press, Knightstown, Indiana. Used by permission of the Bookmark.

Christian Lesher's Farm:
Christian & Catherine bought the land in 1808 from Charles Shull. The farm at the time of the 1869 printing was owned by their son, John Lesher, the parents having dier prior to that date.

Ringgold Meetinghouse:
The Ringgold Meetinghouse (Brethren in Christ) was built in 1871, afew years after the death of Christian & Catherine Lesher. The graveyard in which they are buried was in existence before the meetinghouse was built. The meetinghouse is located immediately east of the graveyard, less than a mile from the Maryland border.

Mt. Alto:
The Christian Lesher farm was identified as being north, not south, of Waynesboro by a reference in a deed stating that the Lesher farm was "bordered by the road leading to Mt. Alto."

Sister Churches:
The German Baptist Brethren and the Mennonites were closely related in faith and practice to the Brethren in Christ. The Antietam German Baptist Brethren meetinghhouse was built in 1795, and the Reformed Mennonite church in the 1830s.

Washington Township

A. *The black inset above indicates the portion of Washington Township represented in the map at right.*

MAP 4

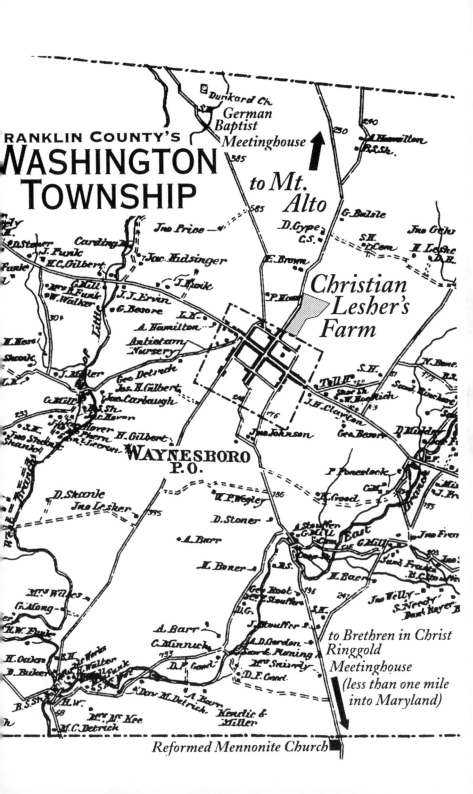

for the price of $262.45.[102] These acres lay adjoining the Lesher
farm or "plantation," as it was sometimes called. The next year they
sold a tract of three acres and seventy-nine perches to John and
James Clayton of Waynesboro for $279.50.[103] Apparently this tract
was taken from the southern panhandle of the Lesher farm.

This transaction establishes that the Christian Lesher plantation
lay north of Waynesboro, because the location of the acres involved
is described as bordering on the road leading from Waynesboro to
Mont Alto (Mont Alto is north of Waynesboro) and bordering on the
"Catholic Church ground."[104] In 1821 the Roman Catholic Church
building was located on the northern edge of Waynesboro, but was
later relocated on Main Street in Waynesboro.[105] The Lesher farm
located south of Waynesboro, sometimes believed to have been the
original Christian Lesher farm, was bought by Christian Lesher's son
John in 1862 for $12,000. It adjoined the Turnpike Road and
consisted of one hundred and thirty-two acres, fifty-six perches.[106]

In 1822 the Leshers bought sixty-four acres and thirty-six
perches in Guilford Township, Franklin County, for $2,633.22.[107]
Four years later they sold one and three-fourths acres and thirty-eight
perches to James Coughran for $147.17.[108] In 1833 they sold one
acre and eighty-four and a half perches to Samuel Gipe for $76.46.[109]
The last two plots were taken from the Lesher homestead. In 1839
the Leshers bought from John Stamey two tracts of land—forty-three
acres of cultivated land, and nine acres and one hundred and forty
perches of mountainous land—for $3,436.87. Both tracts were in
Washington Township; the latter apparently bordered the Lesher
farm.[110] The last purchase of land by the Leshers, made in 1843 and
located in Antrim Township, was obtained for $2,850 and consisted
of one hundred and thirty-eight acres and seventy-four perches.[111]

Christian Lesher's Franklin County tax record gives some insight
into his farming.[112] He began in 1808 with two horses and two cows,
and peaked at six horses and five cows. The number of animals
decreased as Christian's sons appear on the tax lists. His son John
is first listed in 1833 as having one cow; son Henry appears in 1840
with three horses and two cows.[113]

Franklin County

Christian Lesher's Tax Record

year	name		acres	horses	cows	assess.	tax
1808	Lesure, Christian		150	2	2	1684	5.56
1809	Lesher, Christian (weaver)		150	2	2	1590	3.82
1810	"	"	"	"	"	2190	5.72
1811	"	"	"	"	3	2196	7.91
1812	"	"	"	3	3	2214	7.31
1813	"	"	"	2	2	2144	12.79
1814	"	"	"	3	3	9192	13.79
1815	no data						
1816	no data						
1817	Lesher, Christian		"	2	4	7300	10.95
1818	"	"	"	3	3	7395	11.09
1819	"	"	"	2	3	5605	11.21
1820	"	"	"	3	4	5530	8.29
1821	"	"	"	"	4	5515	8.37
1822	"	"	"	4	4	5410	10.82
1823	"	"	"	4	3	5250	10.80
1824	"	"	"	4	4	5410	10.82
1825	"	"	"	3	"	3895	9.73
1826	"	"	"	"	"	3914	8.61
1827	"	"	"	4	3	3900	8.58
1828	"	"	"	"	5	4240	9.33
1829	"	"	"	"	3	4056	8.92
1830	"	"	"	5	5	4150	6.23
1831	Lecher	"	"	"	4	2627	9.20
1832	"	"	"	"	5	2840	11.36
1833	"	"	"	"	4	2948	13.27
1834	Leasure	"	"	"	3	2499	8.75
1835	Lesher	"	"	6	3	2586	6.45
1836	"	"	"	"	4	2540	8.89
1837	Lashure	"	"	?	3	32.54	11.28
1838	Lesher	"	"	2	2	32.06	11.21
1839	"	"	"	"	3	3240	14.58
1840	"	"	200	3	3	4915	19.66
1841	Laesher	"	200	1	"	8376	8.37
1842	"	"	200	"	2	9160	——
1843	"	"	200	"	3	8432	——
1844	Lesher(tenant)		0	1	1	32	——
	(year of retirement)						

1845	"	"	0	1	1	——	——
1847	"	"	0	1	2	——	——
1854	Leisure	"	0	1	2	——	4.68
1855	Lesher	"	0	1	2	——	4.68

A unique aspect of Christian Lesher's occupation as a farmer was his plow. An 1887 source suggests that he brought the plow with him when he moved to Franklin County.[114] It has gained some visibility from being on display at the American history building of the Smithsonian Institute in Washington, D.C. for several decades. Donated to the Smithsonian by Daniel G. H. Lesher, a descendant of Bishop Lesher,[115] it is not identified as Christian Lesher's property but is accompanied by this plaque: "Pennsylvania Plow: This is typical of the 18th century Pennsylvania plows except that it turns the furrow to the left. It is a bar-share plow—so called because the share and the iron bar on the land side are forged together into one unit."

The plow may have been made by Lesher but more likely by some local blacksmith. According to a Mr. Sharrar of the Smithsonian staff in 1968, oxen were used to pull the plow, but this is unlikely in the case of Christian Lesher because he owned horses. (According to Sharrer, oxen were used because they were stronger than horses and could be eaten after their harness days were over.) The blade did not cut deeply into the soil, not being constructed for deep plowing (the value of such plowing was discerned later in the nineteenth century). The wooden moldboard meant that the ground was not turned over with the same finesse as achieved by the use of contemporary steel moldboards.

Sharrer stated that Lesher's plow could be identified as coming from the late eighteenth century because, in addition to oral tradition of the Lesher family, certain construction features place it as belonging to that period. These features include the use of wooden pegs and the type of metal screw. More to the point, around 1800 certain inventors, including Thomas Jefferson, were making advances in plow construction, including more scientifically constructed moldboards and using cast iron for the blade and moldboard. The Lesher plow does not incorporate these advances.[116]

As a farmer, Christian Lesher was naturally much interested in the weather. Recordings of unusual weather events are made in his

Two views of Christian Lesher's plow

Froschauer Bible.[117] (The handwriting of these entries is different
from that in Lesher's writings, thus another person may have
chronicled the events.) Among the entries are the following notes:
"In 1827 on the 2nd of June there was so much frost that much fruit,
rye, and field corn froze and on the 12th, 18th and 23rd there was
frost"; "In 1833 on November 13 thousands of stars fell from 12
o'clock till daybreak"; "In 1836 there was no harvest so we didn't
harvest more actually than the seeds"; "In 1844, 16th April one has
already seen ears of corn." [118]

Christian and Catherine Lesher retired from farming in 1844. In
that year they sold the first land they had purchased (one hundred
and fifty-one acres less sold plots) to son John for $6,600, the forty-
three-acre tract, and the nine-acre mountainous land to son Henry for
$3,320, and one hundred and thirty-eight acres and four perches in
Antrim Township to son Jacob for $3,320.[119]

Also in 1844 Christian and Catherine entered into an agreement
with their oldest son John regarding their retirement needs for the
remaining years of their "natural lives." It was agreed that for the
rest of their days the parents were to have the use of the "brick
dwelling house" and "any other buildings they may occupy" located
on the "plantation." John was responsible to provide "sufficient
stabling for one horse creature and two cows," taking good care of
the animals for as long as the parents lived, with the exception that
the horse needed to be stabled only to the death of Christian should
Catherine live longer than her husband (which she did). John was
also to take care of the horses of visitors, including the steeds of
church members when church services were held at the brick
dwelling house. In addition, the parents were to have "the privilege
to keep one hog" yearly bought at "about the age of six months."
John was to "feed and water said pig until it is about eighteen months
old." They were to pay for the "fatning [sic] expenses of said hog."
Further, they were to have one-third of the chickens raised on the
farm and one-third of the eggs laid. At the same time they had to
provide one-third of the feed for the chickens during the winter
season. They were to have access to one-third of the garden, which
John was "to supply with manure when necessary." Christian and
Catherine had the right to "reserve as much fruit of all kinds" as they
deemed necessary. And John was to "deliver to the house a

sufficiency of fire wood of a good quality cut and split suitable for stove or otherwise as may be required."

Provision was also made for the farm. Twelve hundred dollars was to remain in the tract until 1857 or until the death of both parents. The interest of five percent on that amount was to be paid annually (on the first day of April) to Christian and Catherine as long as they lived. On their death, the $1200 was to be distributed among the children, with John receiving $200, the remaining $1,000 being shared equally among the other children. Finally, John was not to sell the farm as long as his parents lived.[120]

Christian Lesher as a Church Leader

Our knowledge of Christian Lesher's ministry is limited. He informs us that he was converted in 1803 at the age of twenty-eight and, as already noted, was chosen bishop in 1825.[121] The context of his election to the bishopric, according to one account, is that the York County bishop originally had oversight of the Brethren living west of the Susquehanna River. With an increasing number of members moving to Franklin County, it was thought that additional leadership was needed. Thus Lesher was elected as the first resident Brethren in Christ bishop in Franklin County.[122]

To fully understand Lesher as a church leader, including his thought, it is necessary to have some knowledge of River Brethren beginnings and of the three-way division that took place in the group in the mid-1800s. Following a brief sketch of these events, consideration will be given to the following subjects: first, a statement on church discipline by the Brethren in the United States to their counterparts in Canada; second, the origin of the Old Order River Brethren; third, a controversy dealing with marriage and the interpretation of Leviticus 18. All three items involved Lesher as a church leader.

Soon after the middle of the eighteenth century, a pietistic-inspired awakening began among the Pennsylvania Germans and continued through much of the last half of the eighteenth century. The awakening emphasized the necessity of a crisis, heart-felt regeneration experience that bore the fruit of assurance, a personal relationship with God, and living a holy life. Many of the converts began meeting in informal groups for edification and mutual support. Such groups in Lancaster County were identified by location—thus the "Conestoga Brethren," the "Pequea Brethren," and the "River Brethren."[123]

In time (around 1800) most of these groups developed into the United Brethren denomination. The River Brethren, however, remained separate because they believed not only that the regeneration experience was followed by holiness but also that the Bible called for a believers church, as set forth in the New Testament. For the River Brethren, the church was not something that gradually evolved for functional purposes and individual edification, as believed also by the United Brethren; the church was to be established as a body integral to true Christianity. Both the new heart *and* the new community were a part of God's plan for salvation. Christ lived, died, and arose not only to make provision for personal salvation but also to provide for harmonious group living. Such an approach meant that as a group gathered and covenanted with each other, the church modeled its corporate life after the pattern of the New Testament church. Accordingly, the River Brethren became a distinct body earlier (around 1780) than the United Brethren.[124]

The new fellowship was known as the River Brethren because the members lived next to the Susquehanna River and because the newly converted felt a sense of spiritual kinship with others who had the same inner experience. It was a rather common pietist practice to call those who had the experience as brothers and sisters, and the group as brethren. The basis for the familial language—sister, brother, family, household—was the New Testament. Such language was also used in the Anabaptist movement: the word brethren was self-designated in several strands of early Anabaptism.[125]

The Brethren by the river accepted their name, thus becoming known as the River Brethren until the mid-nineteenth century when there occurred a three-fold division of the progressives, moderates and conservatives. (The informal title, River Brethren, continued and continues to be used in some settings, although technically incorrectly.) Few details are available regarding the sequence of events; even the dates involved in the parting of the ways are uncertain. An early twentieth-century history of the Brethren in Christ written for the group states that the conservative schism (Old Order River Brethren) took place around 1843, and the separation of the progressives (United Zion's Children or Brinserites) occurred around 1852.[126] Recent research finds limited support for the 1843 date but has discovered information placing both schisms in the 1850s.

A common reading of the succession of events is that the schisms were interrelated. The crisis began when the parent body, the River Brethren, first warned (in 1853) and then excommunicated (in 1855) an eloquent minister and his followers who had progressive tendencies. The liberal posture of Matthias Brinser (1795-1889) of Dauphin County was shown in his building a meeting house following his refusal to accept the ruling of the Lancaster-York River Brethren leaders not to do so. (Up to this time the River Brethren worshiped in homes and sometimes in schoolhouses.) Brinser and those who followed him gave themselves the name United Zion's Children (now the United Zion Church). By 1855 they were well under way as a new body of believers.[127]

The conservative response, largely from York County (thus one of their names—Yorkers) was led by Bishop Jacob Strickler, Jr. (1788-1859). These Brethren were deeply concerned not only with the meetinghouse innovation but also with "some gradual changes that were creeping in."[128] Whether they broke away from the moderate group (mostly in Lancaster County) before or after the excommunication of Brinser has not been fully documented, but it appears that they departed shortly after Brinser was expelled.[129]

Given the available data, there is no evidence that Christian Lesher was directly involved in the emergence of the United Zion's Children. He was engaged, however, in the issues giving rise to the Hooverites, so-called because they were followers of River Brethren bishop Christian Hoover. The Hooverites made common cause with the Old Order River Brethren and became that group's Franklin County wing.[130]

The moderates continued using the name River Brethren until the American Civil War when, needing to secure legal recognition as a church committed to nonresistance, they registered with the federal government (possibly in 1863) under the name Brethren in Christ.[131]

The Brethren and Discipline

Among the Christian Lesher papers is a two-and-a-half page statement entitled and dated "April 8, 1844."[132] The statement came from a Brethren council meeting held in Donegal, Lancaster County, and was addressed to the Canadian Brethren (then known as Tunkers) who had requested counsel on church discipline. (The Brethren in the two countries were not together as the same body until 1879.)[133]

While no names are affixed to the statement, the penmanship appears to be Lesher's. The choice of words and sentence structure are similar to his, thus at least he was probably involved in crafting the statement that was corporately determined.

The statement begins with a greeting, modeled in part on one used by the Apostle Paul: the Brethren "wish much grace, love, and peace" from God the Father working through "Jesus Christ, our Chief Shepherd and Overseer over the church . . . [and] through the power and working together of the Holy and good Spirit." The statement then proceeds to address the proper handling of a person against whom complaints have been made and who has been brought before the church to determine whether he should remain a member. (The United States Brethren strongly stressed the need for a fair and balanced hearing and decision.) The statement emphasizes the Old Testament imperative of righteous judgement without bias against the poor or in favor of the mighty (Jer. 19:15) and the necessity of having two or three witnesses to establish the truth (Deut. 19:15-20). Diligence and care are to be exercised in discerning the facts and in the judgement made.

The statement establishes the continuity between the two testaments and the fulfillment of the Old in the New Testaments by reference to the words of Jesus that he came not to destroy the law and the prophets but to fulfill them (Mtt. 5:17). The fulfillment is especially found in Matthew 18:15-17, where Jesus indicates that the first step in a case of a difference between persons is to be a one-on-one interaction. The second step, if this first one does not succeed, is for two or three persons (as stated in both Testaments) to call on the one in question. The second step failing, the third is to bring the person before the church (the church is seen as the equivalent of the fulfillment of the Old Testament priest and judge).

The Matthean procedure, the statement indicates, is to be applied within the church and used in instances of sins of weakness, or when words are spoken and deeds done that have not been thought through. When the church meets to hear the case, the positions of both the accuser and the accused are to be evaluated because either one of the two could be at fault. If "God's order and plan" is carried out with diligence and caution, the statement insists, both the accuser and the accused will realize, when they hear the decision of the church, that any fault is theirs, not the body of Christ. After the decision has been made, the guilty person is brought before the church and informed of his sin (according to I Tim. 5:20,21). If the offender repents, he is forgiven and brought back into the fellowship, otherwise he is to be seen as a heathen and a publican.

The Brethren believed in two levels of discipline, although the point is not explicitly made in the statement. To be seen as a publican and sinner did not mean excommunication, since Jesus had interaction with the heathen and publicans (a means by which to correct their understanding of the faith). Those found guilty of lesser sins were usually not given the holy kiss, nor allowed to take communion or wash feet and to participate in council meetings.

However, if the person was clearly guilty of a major sin or his sin became public knowledge (I Cor. 5:11), it was not necessary to follow the three steps of Matthew 18. The guilty one is to be dealt with "immediately by common counsel and judged according to God's judgment," which has already condemned the offender. Several Brethren are to inform the sinner of the decision made against him. In other words, in such a clear-cut case, there was no need for congregational consideration. The guilty person is to be put out of the church according to I Corinthians 5:11-13. If, however, the sinner repents and is ready to confess his sin, he is to be brought before the congregation to make his confession.

The closing paragraph of the statement indicates that the counsel sent to Canada a year earlier not having been adequate for some Canadian Brethren, the Brethren in the United States have reconsidered the matter in the presence of God and through a further study of his Word. This statement is the counsel God would have them give. The document ends with a request that it be read, or heard read, by all in the Canadian church.

The interpretation and application of church discipline was an ongoing concern of the Brethren in Christ. The counsel given the Brethren in Canada was an effort at reaching a common mind on church discipline. The Brethren believed that God reveals his will to the body of believers gathered around the Word and guided by the Holy Spirit. (Lesher's fuller understanding of church discipline will be considered in a later chapter.)

Old Order River Brethren Origins, Marriage, and Leviticus Eighteen

The earliest information in this study on the division that created the Old Order River Brethren and involved Christian Lesher indicates that the issue was the view of Lesher and other Brethren that John Hess of Franklin County should be excommunicated for having married a "close blood relative" or engaged in some sexual act contrary to Leviticus 18.[134] (The key verse was Lev. 18:6. Chapter 20 was also used.) A council meeting held on April 21, 1851, at the home of Bishop Daniel Engle (1788-1881) near Hummelstown, Pennsylvania, considered Hess's expulsion.[135] (For fuller identification of the persons mentioned in this controversy, see notes.) (The understanding of "close blood relatives" in this context, simply stated, was that when a man and woman married, in some sense they become physically or biologically brother and sister. This meant that a man could not marry his deceased brother's wife or, if he had been married, his deceased wife's sister. This idea can be traced back to the fourth century A.D.)

The decision of the church council was that such marriages should not be allowed, and that the brethren were to testify, warn, and advise against them. John Hess was not to be received back into the church until he "becomes penitent," "expresses sorrow," and "openly confesses" his sin. The confession was to include "a solution of the conflict." If he repented, he would be accepted as a true believer, and the unity of the Spirit would once again be experienced between him and the other members.[136]

Within a few weeks, Bishop Lesher wrote a letter, dated June 2, 1851, to Jacob Riefer and his people, and to Bishop Daniel Engle detailing recent developments in the Hess case.[137] With a "heavy, saddened heart," Lesher was compelled to inform his reader of what had happened at a love feast held at Micha Meyer's place.[138] Prior to the Saturday evening service, two brethren came to Lesher, one by the name of Staub doing the talking, stating that they were instructed to inform Lesher that he was not to "stand up front" at the communion (that is, not to preside or to sit with the ministers), although he would be allowed to take part in the meal (communion).[139] That the senior bishop was not to take an active leadership role in the communion was unusual, but Lesher decided that he would be obedient to the request to the extent he could do so with "a good conscience before God." In the ongoing conversation with the two men, Lesher mentioned having a council meeting regarding John Hess, but he thought that such a meeting should not take place at the love feast. The result was that no announcement was made that a council meeting would be held on the Sunday morning of the love feast.

Much to Lesher's surprise a person came to him in the yard soon after breakfast on Sunday asking him to come to the house, but said nothing about considering the Hess case. When Lesher entered the house he noted only a few brethren present, although later a few entered uninvited. Lesher added that many who remained in the yard would not have agreed with the action subsequently taken. The meeting was led by Micha Meyer, Daniel Sanger, and Christian Huber (almost certainly Bishop Christian Hoover [Huber]).[140] Meyer and Sanger stated that Strickler (undoubtedly Bishop Jacob Strickler, Jr., of York County) and John Flory did not agree with the view taken on marriage (apparently a reference to the April 21, 1851, meeting at Daniel Engle's place) that Leviticus 18 prohibited the marrying of "close blood relatives"; rather the passage referred only to fornication and adultery.[141]

At this point, a "Brother Plum" stated that he was surprised that Strickler and Flory could take this position because clearly Leviticus 18 refers to marriage.[142] As Lesher remembered the discussion, no one except the leaders spoke for the leaders' point of view; at the same time all others who voiced their opinion stated that Leviticus prohibited the kind of marriage under discussion. One person pointed out that no council meeting had been held to excommunicate Hess. Lesher defended his action in excommunicating Hess by insisting that Strickler had openly stated that there was nothing wrong with Lesher putting Hess out of the church.

Lesher's defense of his action was not heeded; leaders of the meeting proposed that Hess did not need to make a confession but only to admit that he had "caused the Brethren grief." When asked if he agreed with the proposed solution, Lesher replied that he did not because he could not defend it before God; Hess had to make a confession. The leaders of the meeting were in "great haste" to end the meeting, so Lesher said that if the congregation wanted to let the matter rest, he was ready to do so. (The German text is not complete in giving Lesher's response because some words were missed in photocopying the document.) Lesher's words were taken by the opposition to mean that Lesher had changed his view, but all that Lesher had in mind was that the discussion of the matter in the meeting they were in would end. A vote was taken on the issue; the decision was in favor of the more lenient treatment.

Lesher continued his letter by reporting that at the recent Sunday meeting Hess expressed his "grief." He reported Hess as saying, "It is almost a year ago that I did something, you perhaps all know what it was, something that has grieved the Brotherhood but I did not think it was an offense, and now I am sorry that I have caused offense to the Brethren, but the deed that I have done is one that I have never been convinced was wrong or improper." On the basis of this statement, Hess was reinstated into the church. At this point in his letter, Lesher mentions that at the council meeting held at the love feast (or some later meeting), he had pointed out that Hess had served as a "juryman in the courts," but that in his statement at the Sunday meeting Hess had made no mention of such service.

Having described these events, Lesher asked for evaluation and advice. He apparently wanted to know (the text is not clear) if the council held during the love feast at Micha Meyer's place was truly a council meeting. He saw the opposition at that meeting as not caring for biblical instruction since they did not allow Plum to read Leviticus 18. Lesher added that most members from Chambersburg and in Maryland who voted with the opposition now know they were mistaken in their vote, and are under tension and in distress. Those from the "other side of Chambersburg" were swept to the opposite side, thus the opposition obtained a majority.

Asking for understanding, Lesher wrote, "And now dear Brethren, consider for yourself how hard it is for us to think of Hess as a dear brother" and have communion with him. The same lack of unity is felt toward those who refuse to listen to God's Word. Lesher ends his letter by asserting that he cannot agree with those who act against the Word of God because what happened to King Saul when he disregarded God's Word (I Sam. 15:23-26) will also come upon them.

Lesher's letter indicates that a serious situation had arisen. The council held at Daniel Engle's place had ruled that John Hess was to be excommunicated if he did not repent and confess. It is not clear from Lesher's letter to Riefer and Engle whether Lesher excommunicated Hess or had spoken about doing so and was planning to call a council meeting to formalize the excommunication. What is obvious from his letter is that there were leaders, apparently including Bishop Christian Hoover, in the Franklin County church who disagreed with the need to excommunicate Hess, and that Leviticus dealt with adultery and fornication, not with supposed "close blood relatives." These leaders demoted Lesher, at least temporarily, rejected the rule made at the council in Daniel Engle's residence, and restored John Hess to full church membership upon Hess's expressing his "grief."

A letter dated May 16, 1853, while not dealing with the Leviticus issue and probably not involving Christian Lesher or any of the Franklin County members, has significance for our understanding of the division that occurred with the formation of the Old Order River Brethren. The letter was sent to Bishop Mattias Brinser of Dauphin County by the Lancaster and York County leaders requesting Brinser to stop erecting a meetinghouse because it will "cause great injury and severe suffering."[143] The importance of the letter is seen in that the first four of the twenty-six signatures on the letter were those of two men who became the leaders of the Old Order River Brethren—Jacob Strickler, Jr., and David Stoner—and two who were leaders in what soon was to be called the Brethren in Christ Church—John Gisch and Jacob Hostetter. Thus as of May 16, 1853, the separation between those who became Old Order River Brethren and those who became Brethren in Christ had not taken place: they were all of the same mind in warning Brinser.[144]

The next known important event took place either before or after May 16, 1853, but before November 17, 1853, as will become apparent. A council meeting was held at the home of Jacob Hykes (or Heicks) across the Pennsylvania-Franklin County line in Washington County, Maryland. Evidence indicates that Bishop Jacob Strickler, Jr., if not presiding, at least played an important role in the meeting. Bishop Christian Hoover, in a letter written on February 10, 1857, in which he reviews the events of the "last 4 to 5 years" leading to the Old Order schism,[145] stated that at the council at Hykes's place it was decided that Meyers and Plum were to be chastised for not walking "according to the doctrines of Christ." Christian Lesher was to be dealt with in the same manner because he "allowed this fault in the church and did not chasten them" (that is, Meyers and Plum).[146]

The reason for and details of the misdeeds of Meyers, Plum, and Lesher are not entirely clear, but the evidence suggests that they were related to the love feast held at Micha Meyers's place a few weeks before Lesher's letter of June 2, where the basic issue was the handling, or mishandling, of John Hess and the interpretation of Leviticus 18. In his letter Hoover indicated that those in the opposition (including those whom he identified as "official Brethren") opposed the actions taken at the Hykes council, claiming that the action was contrary to the Bible and encouraged the five excommunicated individuals (see below regarding the five).

In the unfolding events, another council was held on November 17, 1853, in Franklin County at the residence of John Schenck (or Shenk).[147] The records of the meeting state that the "distant brethren" met with the Franklin County Brethren (distant brethren were very likely Brethren from Lancaster and surrounding counties who had some association with the ruling made at the April 21, 1851, meeting at Daniel Engle's place). This council basically agreed with the decision of the action taken in 1851.

Those who believed that the passage in Leviticus meant that the marriage of close blood relatives was forbidden were allowed to hold their view, while those who held that the passage referred to fornication and adultery could do the same. In the future, however, the marriage of close blood relatives was forbidden and the brethren were to testify and advise against such marriage. Those who did not follow this rule were to be dealt with according to Matthew 18. Past attitudes and actions dealing with the controversy were to be forgotten by both sides and accusations and counter-accusations were to cease. Love and tolerance were to characterize relationships, and housekeeping (discipline) was to be carried on as prior to the conflict.[148]

This ruling can be interpreted in more than one way. It may be seen as an effort at reconciliation. Thus it may have conveyed the meaning that past wrong views of Leviticus 18 are history and that a new beginning among the River Brethren is possible. In other words, change your view and remain within the church that you know. It may be that some of the members were undecided on the issue or that some members could be persuaded to change sides. On the other hand, those fully committed to the fornication-adultery position could see that ruling as ambiguous and contradictory. At the meeting at Daniel Engle's place, that view had been condemned, but now such a view was permissible in the past if in the future the position taken at the April 21, 1851, meeting became normative. It could also be perceived as a move to divide the opposition.

The November 17 council meeting also took action regarding Christian Lesher. "Old Brother Lesher," the document reads, "is to be restored to his place [position] and function in his office and keep house just like he did before, and where there are worship services, Lesher is to be in charge and preside just like he has been doing for many years."

Restoring Lesher to his position attests to the seriousness of the tension among the River Brethren on this issue. It may be that Lesher made a confession of his wrong deed (as determined in the Hykes council) and on that basis was restored, or it may have been that those who restored Lesher thought that no confession was needed.

The next development mentioned in the available sources is reported to have taken place in 1854. According to the tradition recounted in the late 1950s by Simon Myers (a prominent member of the Old Order River Brethren living in St. Thomas, Pennsylvania),

Bishop John I. Gisch, acting for the Conoy-Donegal District, Lancaster County, excommunicated Bishop Christian Hoover and his group for being "too orthodox."[149] In his letter, Christian Hoover seems to say (the text is not clear) that five brethren, of whom he was one, were excommunicated. These five men may have been the five leaders of the emerging Hooverite movement. Hoover further indicated that he made an "open confession" on the issues involved. Whether he was reinstated is not known.

If the date 1854 is only oral tradition, it is subject to questioning. As to the charge that Hoover and his group were "too orthodox," Bishop Gisch was probably not referring to correct theology, as implied in the word orthodox; rather he saw the Hooverites as excessively firm in their commitment to historic faith and practice, especially in relation to separation from the world. Such a view is basically true to historical developments: as noted, the Hooverites became the Old Order River Brethren in Franklin County. Hoover himself wrote that the reason given by those who expelled him was that he and his followers did "not want to keep the council [sic] of the church, but want[ed] to keep to the Gospel."[150]

Hoover's statement needs context. There were two methods of making decisions. One method (Hoover's), after a consideration of the issues, was to give the last word to the "elder bishop[s]." As Hoover saw it, this was making decisions "by the Gospel." The second method, ascribed by Hoover to the Lancaster Brethren, was group centered—coming to decisions by group consensus or majority vote.[151] (A question without answer is whether making decisions by majority vote was taken from the American democratic process. Group consensus was inherent in the Brethren view of the church.)

Following the line of history being traced in this paper, the reason for excommunicating the Hooverites could have been their belief that Leviticus 18 refers only to fornication and adultery. Such an interpretation, however, does not readily relate to the two reasons given above for the expulsion of the Hoover group. At the same time the reasons given may have been "correct language" for the Leviticus question.

If 1854 is the accurate date for the expulsion of the Hooverites, it is clear that they were expelled before the Old Order River Brethren came into being. Such a conclusion is reached because the

Lancaster–York group that warned Brinser in 1853 not to build a meetinghouse expelled him and his followers in the summer of 1855 for doing so. If the two groups, Old Order River Brethren and Brethren in Christ, had separated, they would not have cooperated in excommunicating Brinser.[152]

It has also been stated that the Hoover schism took place some ten years after the Brethren in Christ and the Old Order River Brethren divided.[153] Most historians probing the beginnings of the Hoover movement have not come to that conclusion, rather they have explicitly stated or implicitly suggested that the date of origin has not been documented.[154] If the Old Order River Brethren and the Brethren in Christ split some time between 1855 and 1857, the 1854 date for expelling Hoover and his adherents could have been a possibility but not a certainty. The overall impression gained from the Hoover letter is that he was mentally and spiritually involved in the two councils of 1855. The letter unmistakably reflects Hoover's identification with Bishop Jacob Strickler Jr. and his views.

Mention is made of a council held at Jacob Wenger's residence in Hoover's 1857 letter and in a note in the Christian Lesher papers. Lesher gives the date of April 18, 1855, for the meeting; Hoover refers to the meeting as an Easter council.[155] The objective of the gathering was to dispel misunderstandings and to explain actions taken. An issue, if not the key one, at this Wenger meeting was whether the Hykes council was legitimate. The issue, it appears, turned on which of the two methods (discussed above) to use in making decisions.

The approach taken in the April 18 meeting was to have the "York Brethren" explain what they had done at the Hykes council, and the "Lancaster Brethren" evaluate and make righteous judgment on what had been done. (The designations of these names were written by Christian Hoover, and indicate the growing crystallization of two distinct groups.) In the meeting, Strickler (surely Bishop Jacob Strickler, Jr.) explained how they "kept house" (made decisions) at the Hykes council. Hoover relates in his letter that the explanation was well received. To make this point clear, he stated that Bishop Daniel Engle of the Hummelstown area declared openly that "nobody is to say that the Hykes council was not good."

In the time sequence being followed, the next event—in the summer of 1855—was the excommunication of Brinser, at which point the separation of the Old Order River Brethren had not taken place.

After the council at Jacob Wenger's place, the "opposition" (Hoover's designation for those who opposed him) began again, or continued, to see the Hykes council as not legitimate.[156] They expressed their opinion at a council meeting, attended by "many Brethren," on October 31, 1855 (the location is not named but probably it was held in Lancaster County). Here a statement was written, addressed to the "Brethren from [or of] Franklin County," which declared that the consultation held at Jacob Wenger's place was to stand as a "western decision."[157] Nothing more than this is known of the meeting.

Hoover does not mention the meeting, but after stating that he had heard that some brethren were speaking against the Wenger council (and the Hykes council) he reported that he and some others "visit[ed] and examine[d] them" [official brethren]. They found these officials to be "unfaithful" and not realizing the state of their condition. In response to such unfaithfulness, Hoover and those with him obeyed the word of St. Paul, "Wherefore come out from among them, and be ye separate" (2 Cor. 7:17).[158]

A worthy question is whether Bishop Jacob Strickler, Jr., was a member of the party accompanying Hoover on this visit; that he was not mentioned in the letter suggests that he was not in the group. There is also the question of whether Hoover had been excommunicated by the time he visited the official brethren, or whether his "open confession" restored him to church fellowship.

No information is available to throw light on what was meant by "western decision." The flow of events and the geographical location of the counties point to members in York and Franklin Counties as "western." If so, it was almost certainly an action aimed at those who became members of the Old Order River Brethren.

In summary, the Wenger council did not bring about reconciliation. To rule that this council was to be seen as a "western decision" and for Hoover to excommunicate the "official Brethren" strongly suggests the intensity of the crisis. Hoover may have considered the action of the Wenger council as a western decision to be a fundamentally unbiblical move. Thus after interacting with the officials, he may have thought the only option was to excommunicate them. Other possibilities exist but information is lacking on which to form a firm conclusion.

Confirmation that the division that led to the separation of the Old Order River Brethren was the result of a difference between moderates and conservatives is found in a letter written by David Stoner (1814-1888, later a member of the Old Order River Brethren). In one dated March 27, 1856, written on behalf of the York Brethren and addressed to the Lancaster Brethren, Stoner indicates why the Yorkers broke with the Lancaster group: the latter wanted the "Way" wider than that revealed by Jesus and the apostles. In the councils, Stoner wrote, the York Brethren were criticized for being "too strong" and were not ready "to bear and die" for their brothers and sisters. At the same time, the Yorkers thought that the opposition was "too fleshy." Such being the case, Stoner declared that the York Brethren had no other option than to withdraw from the church. Stoner next summarized the "works of darkness" engaged in by the opposition. They "take part in worldly election[s] . . . go to law before the world, . . . send their children to Sabbath School, . . . take them to places of worldly amusement and pleasure . . . [take] money for solemnizing marriages, . . . teach unscriptural doctrine." In closing his letter, Stoner asked his readers (the Lancaster Brethren) to visit them (the York Brethren) and made a call for such values as humility, self-denial, and meekness.

In addressing his readers as Brethren in a non-polemical and considerate manner, Stoner implies (consciously or unconsciously) that reconciliation is still a possibility. In contrast, the reply from Lancaster County was distancing and blunt. Its point was to inform the York Brethren, certainly Jacob Strickler and John Flory but also all who agreed with them, that they are to stay where they have placed themselves in withdrawing from the church: they had not accepted the rulings of the church, therefore they are no longer Brethren.[159] In a tentative study, Avery Zook suggests that as many as twenty-seven families became part of the Old Order River Brethren in Franklin County and in Washington County, Maryland, although he indicates that data on the subject is very limited.[160]

The data available locates the separation of the Old Order River Brethren from the moderate River Brethren between the summer of 1855 (the excommunication of Brinser) and David Stoner's letter of March 27, 1856. The Hooverite break cannot be so sharply dated. The year 1854, when Bishop Gisch expelled Christian Hoover, is not as solidly based in the sources as the separation of the Old Order River Brethren. Hoover does not give dates in his letter, but the movement of the letter implies that he and those with him separated from the official brethren after the Wenger council in April 18, 1855, if not after the October 31, 1855, meeting. Further it appears that the two separations were distinct from each other, but close in time of occurrence. No information has been found to determine when the Yorker Old Order River Brethren and the Hooverites came together.

Key sources remain the problem. Strong effort needs to be made to find the German originals of Christian Hoover's letter of February 10, 1857, David Stoner's letter of March 27, 1856, and the Lancaster County response to Stoner's correspondence. The original documents would give added integrity to or alter the conclusions drawn from the copies.

This chapter was not written to determine the factors that brought about the divisions among the River Brethren. However, having explored, in the process of delineating the life and times of Christian Lesher, the sources dealing with the divisions, it is appropriate to list the elements brought into focus by this study that were basic to the divisions.

First, the evidence indicates controversy regarding the procedure in making decisions. The Old Order River Brethren followed the pattern of the elder bishop, making the final decision after a discussion of the issues; the Brethren in Christ advocated making decisions by consensus or voting. Yet the difference may not have been as clean cut as just stated. In his letter of June 2, 1851, Lesher implies that he excommunicated John Hess apart from a council meeting. The manner of making decisions appears to have been an issue in determining the legitimacy of a council. The problem may have been that the Brethren had not given adequate attention to the process of decision making. It may also have been that there was not much difference between having the oldest bishop, or bishops, sum up the discussion and a group coming to consensus under some leader other than the oldest bishop.

Second, an issue was how to remain true to the historic biblical faith in the context of a changing and upward-bound society. The Brethren believed that God, in a one-time supernatural revelation found in the Bible, revealed the divine way of living. It was God, in Christ's headship and through the guidance of the Holy Spirit, who led his people through the dangers of the evil world. In contrast , American civilization was based on the idea that properly oriented people will find new and better ways of living. This confident attitude influenced American religious life. Brinser in building a meetinghouse felt its impact; according to David Stoner, the moderate River Brethren experienced the attraction of the Sunday school movement and felt the lure of political elections. The Old Order River Brethren were deeply concerned about a gradual acculturation that came to God's people in a hypnotic-like fashion.

Third, the difference of belief on the issue of Leviticus 18 is difficult to identify with the Brethren in Christ, since there is not a shred of evidence of the controversy among the members anywhere except in the papers of Christian Lesher. It is possible to discount the belief as only Lesher's that in some sense when people marry they become of one blood or biologically brother and sister, except for the action of the council in 1851 affirming Lesher's position.

The Last Years

The controversies and divisions of the River Brethren may have clouded the last years of Christian and Catherine Lesher. It is not known what storms they encountered in the first years of his ministry and there is no evidence to explain how they reacted to and reflected on the crisis of their later lives. Lesher did most of his writing when he retired from farming in 1844 at the age of sixty-nine; the content of his writing must be read within that context.

Unfortunately, there is almost no information on the day-to-day leadership and pastoral work of Bishop Lesher. Given his biblical knowledge, theological insight, leadership talents, spiritual gifts, and pastoral heart, there is reason to believe that he was helpful to a great number of people.

A reference in a Bible indicates that Lesher traveled from his home in Washington Township to near Pleasant Hill in Letterkenny Township to perform the marriage ceremony for Christian Brechbill and Nancy Hoover on December 19, 1844 (the bride was the daughter of Bishop Christian Hoover; the wedding was held in her home).[161] Lesher may also have been the guardian of an orphan girl named Elizabeth Lesher. According to the record, Elizabeth repaid Christian Lesher $237.73 for the costs involved in taking care of her from April 8, 1840, to April 12, 1844.[162] But even here there cannot be certainty since there were two Christian Leshers—the one of this account and another in Antrim Township—who could have been the guardian.

Christian Lesher died in September 6, 1856, having lived eighty-one years, four months, and eleven days.[163] Catherine passed away on February 15, 1865, at age eighty-five years, five months, and twenty-five days.[164] Both were buried in the cemetery located next to the Ringgold Brethren in Christ Meetinghouse.

After Catherine's death, the heirs took legal action acknowledging that John had fulfilled all the responsibilities agreed to between him and his parents. The resulting statement was signed by Henry C. Lesher, Magalena Shank, Christian Lesher, Catherine Miller, Jacob Miller, and Jacob S. Lesher.[165] The women here, as in most legal documents, signed with an X. The usual explanation is that women, being uneducated, could not write. Yet Catherine in her song book wrote that the book was hers (someone could have written for her but no evidence supports that this happened), and she was a student at least long enough to receive a piece of fraktur. It is hardly logical to assume that Catherine could write but not her daughters.

This chapter has dealt with the life and times of Bishop Christian Lesher. Some consideration was given to aspects of Brethren in Christ life that were not directly related to Christian Lesher. The study of the Old Order River Brethren—Brethren in Christ division was germane as the Christian Lesher papers throw light on the subject and Bishop Lesher was directly involved. Other chapters will focus on Lesher's world view and writings.

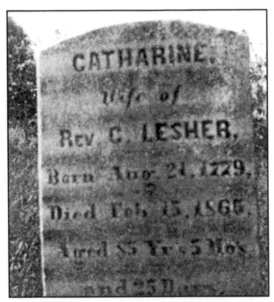

The tombstones of Catherine and Christian Lesher. The markers are located in the cemetery next to the Ringgold Meeting House in Ringgold, Maryland. The photographs are taken from *The History and Genealogical Records of the Strite and Allied Families*, compiled by Carl E. Robinson and Amos W. Strite, 1963.

NOTES

¹C. Henry Smith, *The Mennonite Immigration to Pennsylvania* (Norristown, Pa.: Pennsylvania German Society, 1929), pp. 75-221.

²Robert Proud, *The History of Pennsylvania in North America from Original Institution and Settlement of that Province, Under the First Proprietor and Governor William Penn, in 1681 till after the Year 1742* (Philadelphia: Zachariah Poulson, Jr., 1789), pp. 341-345.

³Ralph B. Strassburger, *Pennsylvania German Pioneers*, William J. Hinke, ed., Vol. 1 (Baltimore: Genealogical Publishing Company, 2nd printing, 1966), pp. 10, 11. Original passenger list, James Good, Philadelphia, September 27, 1727, Pennsylvania State Archives, Record Group 26, Harrisburg, Pa. (hereafter referred to as PSA and RG).

⁴Smith, *Mennonite Immigration*, pp. 183, 184. *Genealogical Register of the Male and Female Descendants of Hans Hege and also the Male and Female Descendants of Henry Lesher and the Relationship Existing Between the Said Two Families* (Chambersburg, Pa.: M. Kieffer and Co., 1859), pp. 5-6.

⁵Daniel R. Lehman, "Bishop Hans Lehman, Immigrant of 1727," *Pennsylvania Mennonite Heritage* (October 1980), p. 16 (hereafter referred to as *PMH*). Will of John Lehman, Lancaster County Will Book Y, Vol. 2, p. 421 (hereafter referred to as LCWB). Letters of David McCormick to author January 15, 1991, and February 1, 1991. Letter of Alex Schmidt to author, one undated but received January 1990. Letter of Mrs. Alex Schmidt to author undated but received in February 1991, and one received August 11, 1994.

⁶Smith, *Mennonite Immigration*, pp. 183, 184. *Genealogical Record, Hege, Lesher*, p. 6.

⁷*Genealogical Record, Hege, Lesher*, p. 5.

⁸Letter of Walter Petto to author, September 3, 1988.

⁹*Mennonite Encyclopedia*, Vol. IV, s.v., "Palatinate," by Gerhard Hein (hereafter referred to as *ME*. When using *ME*, it is necessary to keep in mind that the first four volumes were printed (1955-1959) as a unit, the material covering the alphabet from a to z. The fifth volume, printed in 1990, also covers the range of the alphabet. Thus the citing of the *ME* will always include the volume used). Ibid., s.v., "Pfalz-Zweibrucken," by Maria Klugel and N. van der Zijpp. John L. Ruth, *Maintaining the Right Fellowship* (Scottdale, Pa.: Herald Press, 1984), pp. 25-133.

¹⁰H.S. Bender, "A Swiss Mennonite Document of 1754 Bearing on the Backgrounds of the Origin of the Brethren in Christ," *Mennonite Quarterly Review* (October 1960), 308-309 (hereafter referred to as the *MQR*).

¹¹*ME*, Vol. II, s.v., "Hege," by Christian Hege. Ibid., Vol. I, s.v., "Aargau," by Christian Neff. *Ibid.*, Vol. III, s.v., "Lehman," by Delbert L. Gratz. Letter of Hermann Guth to author, August 20, 1988. Letter of Richard R. Lehman to author, April 22, 1993.

¹²Isaac Zurcher,"Anabaptist-Mennonite Names,"*MQR* (October 1988), 482-485. The names Lesher, Hagy, and Lehman, each with several spellings, are also found in the Palatine Census Lists, for which see Hermann and Gertrud Guth and J. Lemar and Lois Ann Mast, *Palatine Mennonite Census Lists, 1664-1793* (Elverson, Pa.:

Mennonite Family History, 1987), pp. 10-114. *Genealogical Register, Hege, Lesher*, pp. 5,6. Mrs. Alex Schmidt to author, February, 1991. Letter of David McCormick to author, January 15, 1991.

[13]*ME*, Vol. IV, s.v., "Schaffhausen," by Samuel Geiser.

[14]Letter of Hans Lieb to author, January 14, 1988.

[15]For information on French unity, see T. Walter Wallbank et al., *Civilization, Past and Present* (Glenview, Ill.: Scott, Foresman and Co., 1969), pp. 421-426. Ibid., Vol.II, pp 22-31. The quotation regarding the Germanic area of Central Europe is from Donald F. Durnbaugh, comp. and trans., *European Origins of the Brethren* (Elgin, Ill.: Brethren Press, 1958), p. 19. The map of Switzerland is from Ernest Thode, ed., *Atlas for Germanic Genealogy*, 2nd rev. ed., used by permission of Ernest Thode, Heritage House, Ye Olde Genealogie Shoppe, Indianapolis, Indiana.

[16]Letter of Hermann Guth to author, December 12, 1989. Letter of Karge to author, February 4, 1988. Letter of Walter Bohrer to author, December 7, 1988.

[17]Letter of Hermann Guth to author, January 20, 1990. Letter of Lieb to author, August 6, 1991. Letter of Noah Good to author, February 1, 1993. Don Yoder, ed., *Pennsylvania German Immigrants, 1709-1786* (Baltimore: Genealogy Publishing Co., 1980), pp. 329-338.

[18]Letter of Hermann Guth to author, July 17, 1991. Ruth, *Maintaining the Right Fellowship*, p.34.

[19]Letter of Hans Lieb to author, August 6, 1991.

[20]*ME*, Vol I, s.v., "Bern," by Christian Neff and J. C. Wenger; Ruth, *Maintaining the Right Fellowship*, pp. 25-74.

[21]Levi Lukenbach, "Brethren in Christ," *Origin, Confession of Faith and Church Government . . . of the Brethren in Christ . . . 1871-1881* (Wooster, Ohio: Democrat Print, 1881), p. 4.

[22]*ME*, Vol. III, s.v., "Ixheim," by Pierre Sommer and John A. Hostetler. Ruth, *Maintaining the Right Fellowship*, pp. 25-51. Richard McMaster, *Land, Piety, Peoplehood.: The Establishment of Mennonite Communities in America, 1683-1790* (Scottdale, Pa.: Herald Press, 1985), pp. 26-27, 33-35.

[23]Hermann Guth, "Zweibrucken, A City and A Duchy," *Mennonite Family History* (January 1990). 12. *ME*, Vol. IV, s.v. "Zweibruckers," by Harold S. Bender; letter of Hermann Guth to author, December 12, 1989. For an excellent introduction to Mennonite contributions to agriculture in the Palatinate, see Ernst H. Correll, "The Mennonite Agricultural Model in the Palatinate," trans. Marion Lois Luffines, *PMH* (October 1991), 2-13.

[24]*ME*, Vol. II, s.v., "Ernstweiler," by Christian Neff. Letter of Gertrud Guth to author, December 19, 1988.

[25]Letter of Hermann Guth to author, August 20, 1988. Hermann Guth, "The Roggys of Offweilerhof," *Mennonite Family History* (January 1990), 12.

[26]Ruth, *Maintaining the Right Fellowship*, pp. 28, 38-41. MacMaster, *Land, Piety, Peoplehood*, pp. 33,34. *ME*, Vol. IV, s.v., "Pennsylvania," by C. Henry Smith.

[27]*Dictionary of Christianity in America* (1990), s.v., "Friends, The Religious Society of (Quakers)," by R.E. Selleck (hereafter referred to as *DCA*); *Brethren Encyclopedia* (1983), s.v., "Society of Friends," by T. Canby Jones (*Brethren*

Encyclopedia hereafter referred to as *BE*). A bit of history is needed to understand the designation German Baptist Brethren. When the new fellowship or community came into being in Schwarzenau, Germany (1708), the group intentionally did not give itself a distinctive non-biblical name. They simply called themselves Brethren or Baptist-minded (*Taufgesinnten*). Outsiders denominated them by names like Anabaptists, Baptists, New Baptists, Dunkers, etc. Most of the members emigrated to Pennsylvania in the years 1719 and 1729. In 1836 they incorporated, giving themselves the name of Fraternity of German Baptists. That name was altered in 1871 to German Baptist Brethren. The years 1880-1883 was a crisis time for in those years the body divided into three groups. The conservatives became the Old German Baptist Brethren, the progressives the Progressive Brethren, and the moderates, in 1908, the Church of the Brethren. A further division took place among the Progressive Brethren in the years 1939-1940, one wing becoming the Fellowship of Grace Brethren and the other the Brethren Church (Ashland, OH). Mention should also be made of the Dunkard Brethren who left the Church of the Brethren in 1926. Given such developments, my choice of the name, German Baptist Brethren, is somewhat arbitrary. *BE*, s.v., "Names; Brethren," by Donald F. Durnbaugh and Dennis D. Martin.

[28]*BE*, s.v., "Palatinate," by Donald F. Durnbaugh.

[29]Pennsylvania German culture expert, Frederick S. Weiser, has written that the Lutheran and Reformed church people "probably constituted 90%" of the Pennsylvania German church people. This means that the emigration of Brethren and Mennonites was part of a much larger movement. *The Gift is Small, the Love is Great: Pennsylvania German Small Presentation Frakturs* (York, Pa.: York Graphic Services, Inc., 1994), p. 9. Martin H. Schrag, "The Brethren in Christ Attitude Toward the 'World'" (Unpublished Ph. d. diss., Temple University, 1967), pp. 9-10.

[30]The oath was required in part because too many undesirable people (in poor health and of questionable morals) were entering the colony, and in part because a large number were from foreign countries, especially Germany and Switzerland. The oath was instituted in 1727, meaning that immigrants on the boat bringing the Lesher, Lehmans, and Heges were among the first to take the oath. Since Anabaptists refused to swear an oath, they were allowed to affirm. See H. Egle, ed., *Pennsylvania Archives*, 2nd Series, Vol. XVII (Harrisburg, Pa.: Commonwealth of Pennsylvania, 1890), pp. 3-4.

[31]*Genealogical Register, Hege, Lesher*, p. 5. When they arrived, the area was still a part of Donegal Township, Rapho Township being carved out of Donegal Township in 1741. Manheim was named after the town of the same name in Germany, and Rapho after the parish of Rapho in Donegal Township, Ireland. Franklin Ellis and Samuel Evans, *The History of Lancaster County, Pennsylvania, With Biographical Sketches of Many of its Pioneers and Prominent Men* (Philadelphia: Everts and Peck, 1883), p. 1125.

[32]John L. Ruth, "The Earth is the Lord's": A Narrative History of the Lancaster Mennonite Conference (Unpublished manuscript in the possession of the Mennonite Historical Society, 1991), p. 258.

[33]*ME*, Vol. III, s.v., "Manheim," by Ira D. Landis. A study was made by John W.W. Loose, president and editor of the Lancaster County Historical Society, of the

1790 United States Census along the line of national and ethnic surnames. He found that in Rapho Township as of 1790, 213 household heads (in effect families) were German, 17 were English, 25 Scottish, 1 Welsh, 3 Huguenots, no Irish, no Jews, and 11 slaves. Apart from the slaves, the above numbers mean that 82.5% of the settlers in Rapho were German. Undated sheet attached to letter of John W.W. Loose to the author, March 5, 1991. John Loose interview with Dorothy A. Schrag, June 2, 1994.

[34]David J. Cuff et al., eds., *The Atlas of Pennsylvania* (Philadelphia: Temple University Press, 1989), p. 82.

[35]PSA, RG-17, Survey Book A46-239, Patent Book A15-473.(Hereafter Survey Book is referred to as SB and Patent Book as PB).

[36]Ibid., SB C105-232, PB A12-81. Also Martin G. Weaver, *Mennonites of Lancaster County Conference* (Scottdale, Pa.: Mennonite Publishing House, 1931), p. 181.

[37]PSA, RG-17, SB C112-167, PB AA8-76.

[38]Lancaster County Historical Society Library, Lancaster County Tax Records, 1750-1855, Rapho Township, 1751-1825. (Hereafter Lancaster County Historical Society Library is cited as LCHSL, Lancaster County Tax Records as LCTR, and Rapho Township Tax Lists as RTTL.)

[39]Lancaster County Archives, LCWB Y, Vol. 2, p. 405. "The Last Will of Henry Lesher, Translated" (1784), trans. Peter Miller (Lancaster County Archives hereafter cited as LCA.)

[40]Ibid.

[41]*Genealogical Register, Hege, Lesher*, p. 9. Ronald E. Lesher, Sr., "Henrich and Maria Lesher: Notes on a First Generation Family" (Unpublished paper, Quakertown, Pa.: Reproduced by the author, 1985), pp. 1-4. Carlton O. Wittlinger, *Quest for Piety and Obedience: The Story of the Brethren in Christ* (Nappanee, Ind.: Evangel Press, 1978), pp. 17-25. See also Owen H. Alderfer, "The Mind of the Brethren in Christ: A Synthesis of Revivalism and the Church Conceived as Total Community" (Unpublished Ph.D. diss., Claremont Graduate School, 1964), pp. 30-49. E. Morris Sider, *The Brethren in Christ in Canada, Two Hundred Years of Tradition and Change* (Nappanee, Ind.: The Canadian Conference, Brethren in Christ Church, 1988), pp. 7-8. Samuel S. Wenger et. al., eds., *A Foundation Book of the American Wengers* (Lancaster Pa.: Pennsylvania German Heritage History, 1978), pp. 101-116.

[42]Last Will of Henry Lesher. The will was probated on March 31, 1784.

[43]Letter of David A. McCormick to the author, July 25, 1990.

[44]PSA, RG-17, SB C112-159, PB 8-76.

[45]PSA, RG-47; LCTR 1750-1855, RTT12, 1751-1825.

[46]On the inner side of the back cover of Christian Lesher's Sauer Bible is a listing of the death and life span of sixteen persons, all related to the Christian Lesher family. The item contains the information that Henry Lesher, Jr. "died November 7, 1821, age 81 years three months and seven days." Next on the list is Frena (Zedy) Lesher who "died on July 6, 1804, age sixty years." For the total listing, see Appendix B.

[47]*Genealogical Register, Hege, Lesher*, p. 39. Letter of Robert J. Zetty to the author, January 29, 1990. Peter Zetty and family moved from Lancaster County to the Hagerstown, Maryland area (immediately south of Franklin County,

Pennsylvania), and later to the Harrisonburg, Virginia, area. Will of Jacob Zedy in German original, LCA, LCWB J, Vol. 1, p. 385. English translation in LCA, LCWB X, Vol. 2, p. 112. In the three-volume work, Strassburger, *Pennsylvania German Pioneers*, mention is made of only one Zedy in the thousands of Germans emigrating to Pennsylvania (vol. 2, p. 484). This was Abraham Zety who arrived in Philadelphia on September 23, 1752. Since the name had variant spellings, all listings beginning with Ze, Zi, Ce, and Ci were examined. Even so, other spellings may have been used.

[48]Letter of Robert J. Zetty to author, January 29, 1990. See also Petitions of Peter Zedy, one dated November 7, 1759, the other the "first Tuesday of March 1760," in LCHSL, "Orphan Court Minutes", Misc. Files 2, 1760. Wilmer J. Eshleman, "The River Brethren Denominations," *Papers of the Lancaster County Historical Society*, Vol. LII, No. 7 (1948), p. 180. LCA, LCWB, B, Vol. 1, p. 219.

[49]Ibid., Report of Jacob Cauffman, John Hare, Samuel Hare, Mathias Blasser [one name not legible], March 4, 1760.

[50]LCA, Lancaster County Deed Book L, Vol. I, pp. 231-234 (Lancaster County Deed Book hereafter cited as LCDB). John E. Engle and Eugene K. Engle, "A Letter from Immigrant Ulrich Engel to Switzerland in 1755," *PMH* (July 1993), 16-18.

[51]Ibid.

[52]*United States Direct Tax of 1798—Tax Lists for the State of Pennsylvania*, Rapho Twp., pp. 260-161, LCHSL. A Welsh Quaker, upon seeing hardworking and industrious German farmers operating in Pennsylvania, wrote, "It is pretty to behold our back settlements, where the barns are as large as palaces, while the owners live in log huts; a sign, though, of thriving farms," quoted in John L. Ruth, *'Twas Seeding Time: A Mennonite View of the American Revolution* (Scottdale, Pa.: Herald Press, 1976), p. 21. Another item of interest regarding the inception of the Brethren in Christ is whether the Peter Witmer who married Ulrich Engel's oldest child, Catherine, was also the Peter Witmer who was appointed, July 2, 1764, to be the guardian of Ulrich Engel's youngest child, Jacob, and the Peter Witmer who agreed with Jacob Engel (probably in the 1770s) that believers immersion baptism was the biblical mode of baptism. Dr. Phillip E. Bedient, Witmer genealogy specialist, believes that only one Peter Witmer was involved. It is known there was more than one Peter Witmer living in the area; the limited research engaged in this study supports the view of Dr. Bedient. Letter of Bedient to author, April 13, 1994. From the letter we also learn that Peter Witmer arrived in Philadelphia on December 22, 1744. Eshleman, "River Brethren Denominations," pp. 178-182. Wittlinger, *Quest for Piety and Obedience*, pp. 22-23. John K. Miller, "The River Brethren," *The Pennsylvania-German* (January, 1906), p. 17. Personal interview with Phillip Bedient, July 19, 1994. Pennsylvania State Archives, Record Group 4, Military Accounts, Militia 1777-94, Lancaster County rolls, 169-175. (Hereafter Pennsylvania State Archives, Record Group will be referred to as PSA, RG.)

[53]Martin H. Schrag, "Henry Lesher Jr. and the American Revolution," *Brethren in Christ History and Life* (December 1995), 382-395 (hereafter referred to as BICHL). *Genealogical Register, Hege, Lesher*, pp. 40-41. Thomas Montgomery, ed., *Pennsylvania Archives* 5th series, vol. VII (Harrisburg, Pa.: Commonwealth of Pennsylvania, 1906) pp. 213, 695, 717, 744, 762, 788, 793. Daniel R. Lehman,

Mennonites of the Washington County, Maryland and Franklin County, Pennsylvania (Lititz, Pa.: Publication Board of the Eastern Pennsylvania Church and Related Areas, 1990), pp. 11-12. Letters of Daniel R. Lehman to author, February 2, 1991, and June 22, 1991. Daniel R. Lehman, comp., "Descendants of Orphan Henry Lesher" (Unpublished genealogy, 1994), pp. 1-5. Interview with James Lesher, May 26, 1994.

[54]A.W. Climenhaga, *History of the Brethren in Christ Church* (Nappanee, Ind.: E.V. Publishing House, 1942), p. 71.

[55]Note of Christian Lesher recorded on the inside of the last sheet of his Sauer Bible. His Sauer Bible was located in the Kittochtinny Historical Library, Chambersburg, Pennsylvania. For information regarding the Sauer Bible see page 82. Carl E. Robinson and Amos W. Strite, comp., *The History and Genealogical Records of the Strite and Allied Families* (Hagerstown, Md.: Amos Strite, 1963), pp. 1, 657. According to George A. Seilhamer the Strite family was Mennonite at the time of emigration. See Seilhamer, ed., *Biography Annals of Franklin County, Pennsylvania* (Chicago: The Genealogical Publishing Co., 1905), pp. 556-557. The parents of Catherine lived in Lancaster County on a farm located partly in Lancaster County and partly in Dauphin County. Catherine's older brother moved to Franklin County at some point in his life.

[56]LCTR 1750-1855, RTTL 1751-1829. *United States Tax of 1798*, pp. 128, 169.

[57]In the material researched no primary or fully convincing secondary source was found regarding the year Christian and Catherine Lesher moved to Franklin County. It is known, as documented in this article, that Christian was on the Rapho Township tax lists until 1806, and that he bought land in Franklin County in 1808. The date of 1807 is given in *History of Franklin County, Pennsylvania* (Chicago: Warner, Beers, and Co., 1887), p. 949.

[58]LCA, LCWB P., Vol. 1, pp. 208, 209. Ronald Lesher, p. 2. Ronald Lesher also stated that his uncle, Christian Lesher, lived on the old homestead in Rapho Township, where he died in 1828.

[59]*United States Tax List of 1798*, pp. 128, 169.

[60]Fraktur piece in Lesher's Sauer Bible, Kittochtinny Historical Society Library. Letter of Noah Good to author, August 12, 1991, p. 20. Letter of Frederick S. Weiser to author, November 12, 1991. Gerald C. Studer, *Christopher Dock: Colonial Schoolmaster* (Scottdale, Pa.: Herald Press, 1967), pp. 189, 190.

[61]The tulip was one of the most frequently used motifs in Pennsylvania Dutch folk and fraktur art. Fraktur writing was an ornate style of broken or fractured writing featuring decorative motifs, expanded with intricate flourishes, and often illuminated in brilliant colors, most often in red, green and black. The beginnings of the style reach back into early medieval times as monks in monasteries hand-copied manuscripts to further learning and spirituality. The introduction of printing in the fifteenth century resulted in a gradual decline of the art of hand-illumination, but it continued in folk art throughout much of Western Europe. The German settlers who came to Pennsylvania from southern Germany and Switzerland (upper Rhine area) brought with them the medieval manuscript writing in its folk art form, and creatively invigorated and modified it given their Pennsylvania experience. Fraktur art was used to embellish and decorate religious poems, baptismal

certificates, songs and other writings. It became a means of fostering heart-centered religion and upright, pious living.

Frederick S. Wiser states that the kind of fraktur given to Catherine Lesher was an example of Small Presentation frakturs. He describes the category as "usually about one-eighth of a sheet of colonial . . . paper about four inches by six," usually featuring birds and/or flowers, and their use in part due to Christopher Dock recommending the practice of rewarding excellent school work with the gift of a small fraktur piece. *The Gift is Small, the Love is Great*, pp. 13-14.

Finally, it was not very common for "plain people," such as Mennonites and Amish, to put signs and designs on such objects as barns, chairs, chests, and tombstones, but many were receptive, especially school teachers, to fraktur writings and art. Mennonite historian John Ruth has written regarding fraktur art: "What is interesting is that this is one of the few folk-arts that was affectionately espoused by the Mennonites and found useful for religious purposes." Ruth, *Maintaining the Right Fellowship*, p. 167. Studer, *Christopher Dock*, pp. 179-196. Henry Kauffman, *Pennsylvania Dutch American Folk Art*, C.G. Holme, ed. (New York: American Studio Books, 1946), pp. 9-22, 30-32. Frances Lichten, *Folk Art Motifs of Pennsylvania* (New York: Dover Publications, Inc., 1954), pp. 1-32. *Encyclopedia of World Art*, s.v., "Folk Art," by John L. Stoudt, *Pennsylvania Folk Art* (Allentown, Pa.: Schlechter's, 1948), pp. 3-128. *ME*, Vol. IV, s.v., "Pennsylvania-German Cultures," by Arthur D. Graeff.

[62]Translated by Noah Good in letter to author, August 21, 1991.

[63](Germania, 1829). Added to the work, as was common to the *Kleine Davidsche Kalterspiel*, was a forty-eight-page supplement entitled *Die kleine Harfe*.

[64]*BE*, s.v., "Das kleine Davidische Psalterspiel der Kinder Zions," by Hedda Rasckka Durnbaugh. Photocopy of Fraktur piece in Brethren in Christ Archives.

[65]I. Daniel Rupp, *The History and Topography of Dauphin, Cumberland, Franklin, Bedford and Perry Counties* (Lancaster, Pa.: Gilbert Hills, Proprietor and Publishers, 1846), pp. 449-450, 484-485.

[66]Philip S. Klein and Ari Hoogenboom, *A History of Pennsylvania*, ed. and enlarged (University Park, Pa. : Pennsylvania State University Press, 1980), pp. 57-59.

[67]*History of Franklin County*, p. 315.

[68]Ibid., pp. 310-316. M.S. Foltz, "The German Influence in Pennsylvania, with Special Reference to Franklin County, "*The First Year of the Kittochtinny Historical Society* (1900), pp. 62-83. J. Lenwood Eisenberg, ed., *A History of the Church of the Brethren in the Southern District of Pennsylvania* (Quincy, Pa.: Quincy Orphanage Press, 1941, reprinted 1961), pp. 3-10. *ME*, Vol. II, s.v., "Franklin County, Pa.," by J. Irvin Lehman.

[69]An example of change was some Mennonite families becoming Brethren in Christ. Mennonite historian Daniel R. Lehman has mentioned that this was true for such names as Burkholder, Lehman, Rife, Wenger, and Hoover, and that "the River Brethren Church in Franklin county drew its numeric strength from the Mennonites." *Mennonites in Washington County, Franklin County*, p. 70.

[70]Letters of Richard Winger to author, July 8, July 29, and September 6, 1989. Winger bases his conclusions on land deeds and the last will of Abraham Wingert. Seilhamer, *Biographical Annals of Franklin County*, pp. 654-655.

[71]The last year Samuel Betzner was on the Donegal Township (Lancaster County) tax list was 1793. In that year, Samuel Betzner purchased 180 acres and ninety-nine perches ("and allowance of six P"—for roads, etc.) from Phillip Sprecher for the price of 1,300 pounds. The land was located in Greene Township, Franklin County. In 1795 Betzner sold his farm to Peter Miller for 2400 pounds and bought 115 acres and 53 peaches from John Scott (land in Montgomery Township) for 862 pounds and 10 shillings. He sold this farm to Jacob Zook, 100 acres in 1798 and 25 in 1799. As of April 16, 1796 he was living in Maryland where he purchased seventy-two acres in Washington County for 578 pounds. Franklin County Court House, Register and Recorder Office, Franklin County Deed book, No. 3, pp. 25, 293. (Franklin County Court House hereafter cited as FCCH, Register and Record Office as RRO, and Franklin County Deed Book as FCDB.) Ibid., No. 5, p. 26; No. 9, pp. 389, 459, Washington County, Maryland, Deed book, No. 1.9, pp. 611, 612. Author's interview with J. Harold Sherk, December 11, 1987. Sider, *Brethren in Christ in Canada*, p. 13. Schrag, "Attitude Toward the 'World,'" p. 308.

[72]Record of Valuations, No. 3, Franklin County, 1796-1800, MG-4 County Records Collection, Franklin County, Washington Township, 1794, 1796, 1799, 1801-1804.

[73]Samuel G. Sollenberger, *Abram W. Sollenberger Family* (n.p.: 1908), p. 1. Interview with Jacob L. Sollenberger, January 21, 1988.

[74]D. Ray Heisey, "The Force of Narrative: Portrait of Bishop B.F. Hoover," *BICHL* (December 1988), 231-232. Laban T. Brechbill, *History of the Old Order River Brethren*, ed. Myron Dietz (n.p.: Brechbill and Strickler, 1972), pp. 156-157.

[75]Ibid., pp. 156-157. Seilhamer, *Biographical Annals of Franklin County*, pp. 304-305. Abigail H. Strickler et al., *Stricklers of Pennsylvania* (n.p.: The Strickler Reunion Association of Pennsylvania, 1942), p. 4. The Seilhamer and Strickler sources are difficult to integrate.

[76]Letter of Roy Wenger to author, July 8, 1989. Schrag, "Attitude Toward the 'World,'" p. 308. Material regarding John Meyer is written in a family Bible now in the possession of Ernest E. Meyers, Chambersburg, Pennsylvania.

[77]Avery Zook, "What Mean These Bricks? The Story of the Ringgold Meeting House," *BICHL* (April 1992), 21-22.

[78]Letter of Avery Zook to author, June 24, 1992.

[79]Avery Zook, "Martin H. Oberholser: Franklin County Bishop," BICHL (December 1985), 2-5.

[80]Harry D. Zook, *Zug/Zuck/Zouck/Zook Genealogy* (Baltimore: Gateway Press, 1983), pp. 51-55, 195-196, 263-274.

[81]Harry D. Zook states that a third son—John—was a Brethren in Christ minister in Franklin County, but Brethren in Christ historian, Avery Zook, indicates that there is no documentation supporting the view that John was a minister. Letter of Avery Zook to author, June 24, 1992.

[82]Zook, "What Mean These Bricks?" p. 22.

[83]Ibid.

[84]Ibid., pp. 22, 24.

[85]Letter of Avery Zook to author, June 13, 1994.

[86]Zook, "What Mean These Bricks?" p. 24.

[87]Charles C. Boyer, *American Boyers* (Kutztown, Pa.: Kutztown Publishing House, 1915), pp. 341-351. Letter of Charlie B. Byers to author, October 23, 1992.

[88]Goldia Hawbaker Clark and Eliphalet H. Hawbaker, *One Line of Descendants of the Hawbaker Family in America* (n.p.: The Seventh Generation in America Hawbakers, 1958), pp. 6-14. *Hawbaker Descendants from 1737 to 1978*, 2nd ed. (n.p.: n.d.), pp. 12-16. Strassburger, *Pennsylvania German Pioneers*, pp. 188-190. On the passenger list were the following four Hawbaker men—Christian, Joseph, Hans, and Jacob—and four Hawbaker women—Anna, Catarina, Magdalene, and Maria.

[89]The Waldensians was a movement of the twelfth and thirteenth centuries begun by Peter Waldo of Lyons, France. A rich merchant, he came to believe that he was to sell all that he possessed and give the money to the poor, obey the teachings of Christ, especially as given in the Sermon on the Mount, and become a traveling evangelist. The context of his conversion was the wealth, corruption, and political power of the Roman Catholic Church. Waldensians believed in the authority of the Bible, pacifism, non-swearing of oaths, the need to pattern life according to the New Testament church, and the unworthiness of immoral priests. They also rejected the Constantinian linking of church, state, and society, and rejected the Roman Catholic practices that they saw to be contrary to Scripture, such as the teaching of purgatory. At the same time, they did not formally reject infant baptism and attendance at mass; they saw themselves as the yeast in the church, despite that the Roman Catholic Church condemned the movement. Some scholars believe that Anabaptism was indebted to the Waldensians.

During the sixteenth-century Protestant Reformation, the Waldensians were strongly influenced by the Reformed (Calvinistic) movement and became a part of the French Protestant development known popularly as the Huguenots. As a result, they moved from loosely gathered groups led by itinerant ministers to an institutionalized organization led by designated leaders. They constructed their own church buildings and no longer had anything to do with the Roman Catholics. They accepted Reformed theology and identified themselves with Reformed political practices and fortunes, including military service.

Before and after the Protestant Reformation, the Waldensians were persecuted, in part because their geographic base was in the Alps bordering between Italy and France. Wars often caused the boundary line to move so they were variously under the rule of Italy and of France. The Berts who arrived in Chambersburg in 1830 came from Germany, where they had gone to escape discrimination and persecution practiced against them by former European rulers. Eldon F. Bert et al., eds., *A History and Genealogy of Peter Bert to 1987* (Harrisburg, Pa.: Peter Bert Family, Editorial Committee, 1987), pp. 4-39. E. Morris Sider, *Nine Portraits: Brethren in Christ Biographical Sketches* (Nappanee, Ind.: Evangel Press, 1978), pp. 17-19. *The New International Dictionary of the Christian Church* (1974), s.v., "Waldenses," by Peter Toon. *BE*, s.v., "Waldenses," by Murray L. Wagner, Jr.

[90]Climenhaga, *History of the Brethren in Christ Church*, p. 71.

[91]Brechbill, *History of the Old Order River Brethren*, pp. 36, 220.

[92]Photocopy of original provided by David Meyers, Orrstown, Pennsylvania. He also volunteered a second circle chart (see reduced size copy in this end note). The title, in English translation, reads: "Places [of meetings] of Congregations

(*Gemeinde*) North of Chambersburg, 1846." The male names of the two circles are identical, except one John Sollenberger has the middle initial of R and the other B. As can be seen, the names of the women are not on the second chart. Letter, Noah G. Good to author, January 23, 1995.

[93]Kittochtinny Historical Society Library.

[94]Wittlinger, *Quest for Piety and Obedience*, pp. 555-556.

[95]I.H. M'Cauley, *Historical Sketch of Franklin County, Pennsylvania*, 2nd ed. (Harrisburg, Pa.: Patriot Publishing Company, 1878), pp. 263-264. Personal interview with Avery Zook, June 2, 1991.

[96]*History of Franklin County*, p. 315.

[97]Foltz, "German Influence in Pennsylvania," 78.

[98]Zook, "What Mean These Bricks?" pp. 20-25.

[99]The survey document reads as follows: "Beginning at a black Oak thence by land of John Wallace South sixty two degrees [*sic*, hyphens are missing in original document] and fifty six perches and three quarters to a White Oak thence by land of John Cochran North twenty eight degrees East one hundred and twenty four perches to a Hickory South forty four degrees East eighty six perches to a Chestnut Oak North seventy three degrees East twenty nine perches to a White Oak North fifty two degrees East sixty two perches and a half to a Post South fifty three degrees East sixty two perches an a half to a Pine thence by land of John McClenaghan North nineteen degrees West fifty four perches to a Black Oak North fourteen degrees East fifty six perches to a White Oak thence by land of William Bleakley North seventy eight degrees West forty four perches to a Pine South seventy three degrees West sixteen perches to a Pine North seventy two degrees and a half West sixty eight perches to a Hickory North eight degrees West twenty six perches and a quarter to a Pine and thence by land of John Price South thirty seven degrees West two hundred and forty one perches." A perch is a measure of length, five and a half yards, and a measure of size, three and one-fourth square yards. For the survey, see PSA, RG-17, PB P-63, Roll 39, p. 354, and FCCH, RRO, FCDB, No. 8, pp. 205-206.

[100]*BE*, s.v., "Preiss (Price) Family," by Dorothy B. Lapp. *BE*, s.v., "Antietam (Price) Church of the Brethren," by Mary Landis Rice. J. Lindwood Eisenberg, ed., *Church of the Brethren in the Southern District*, pp. 7-9.

[101]*History of Franklin County*, p. 316. Daniel Lehman, *Mennonites in Washington County, Franklin County*, pp. 161, 162.

[102]FCCH, RRO, FCDB, No. 12, pp. 445-446.

[103]Ibid., No. 13, p. 271.

[104]Ibid., D.G. Beers, ed., *Atlas of Franklin County, Pennsylvania* (Philadelphia: Pomeroy and Beers, 1868), p. 53. During the nineteenth century (from 1807 to 1892), the Mont Alto Iron Ore Company was a thriving business. The company owned 22,000 acres of land, worked 17 mines, and employed up to 500 men. *1978 Engagement and Note Calendar* (Waynesboro, Pa.: J. and M. Printing, 1978).

[105]Personal interview with Todd A. Dorsett, Waynesboro, Pennsylvania, February 2, 1988. "History of the Church of St. Andrew, Waynesboro, PA." (Unpublished paper, October 1956), St. Andrew Church, pp. 1-3. *Atlas of Franklin County*, p. 53.

[106]FCCH, RRO, FCDB, No. 36, p. 355. The farm was bought from Jacob Carbaugh.

[107]Ibid., No. 13, pp. 247-248.

[108]Ibid., No. 14, p. 31.

[109]Ibid., No. 16, p. 202.

[110]Ibid., No. 17, p. 572.

[111]Ibid., No. 19, pp. 148-149.

[112]PSA, RG-47, Franklin County Tax Records, 1808-1845. Assess Books, 1847, 1854, 1859. The Assess Books at the time of my using them were located in a basement room of the Franklin County Court House. They were unorganized. I found three for the years following 1845.

[113]PSA, RG-47. Franklin County Tax Records, 1833, 1840.

[114]*History of Franklin County, Pennsylvania*, p. 949.

[115]Personal interview with Pete Daniel, February 10, 1988 and with Francis Gadson, February 19, 1992.

[116][Martin H. Schrag], "The River Brethren and His Plow," *Evangelical Visitor*, September 8, 1968, p. 14. The source is incorrectly identified, and has not been located (editor's note).

[117]*Die Bibel*, Christoffel Froschauer Version, 1538, two unnumbered pages between the Old and New Testaments. The Froschauer Version was favored by believers in the Anabaptist, Mennonite, and Brethren traditions. *ME*, Vol. II., s.v., "Froschauers Bible and Testaments," by Adolf Fluri.

[118]Letter of Noah Good to author, February 1, 1993, trans. Noah Good, pp. 5-6. Kittochtinny Historical Society Newsletter (October 1988), p. 2.

[119]FCCH, RRO, FCDB, No. 19, p. 372. Ibid., No. 21, p. 19. Ibid., No. 19, pp. 313, 314.

[120]Ibid., No. 19, pp. 294-295.

[121]Christian Lescher, *Das kleine geistliche Magazin als ein Zeugniss der Wahrheit; Bestehend in unterschiedlichen Stucken des Christlichen Erkenntnisses* (Chambersburg, Pa.: M. Kieffer und Comp., 1849), p. 3. Climenhaga, *History of the Brethren in Christ Church*, p. 71.

[122]Jacob L. Sollenberger, "Division of the River Brethren in the Mid-1800's" (Chambersburg, Pa.: reproduced by the author, ca. 1960), single sheet. See also Brechbill, *History of the Old Order River Brethren*, pp. 156-158. A. Zook, "What Mean These Bricks?" p. 20.

[123]A Familiar Friend, "History of the River Brethren," *History of all Religious Denominations in the United States* (Harrisburg, Pa.: John Winebrener, 1848), pp. 553-556. Wittlinger, *Quest for Piety and Obedience*, pp. 15-30. Alderfer, "Mind of the Brethren in Christ," pp. 18-49. Schrag, "Attitudes Toward the 'World,'" pp. 11-23.

[124]Wittlinger, *Quest for Piety and Obedience*, pp. 35-37. Alderfer, "Mind of the Brethren," pp. 50-85. Schrag, "Attitude Toward the 'World,'" pp. 24-54, 130-152.

[125]*BE*, s.v., "Pietism," by F.E. Stoeffler. Wittlinger, *Quest for Piety and Obedience*, pp. 26-28. ME, Vol. I, s.v., "Brethren," by Christian Neff and Harold S. Bender.

[126]"Brief History of Brethren in Christ (River Brethren)," *Minutes of General Conference of Brethren in Christ (River Brethren) from 1871-1904* (Harrisburg, Pa.:

Brethren in Christ Church, 1904), pp. 313-314. Wittlinger, *Quest for Piety and Obedience*, p. 134.

[127]S. H. Brinser, H. G. Light, and P. Singer, *Brief History of the United Zion's Children Church* (n.p.: 1917), pp. 1-8. Paul Hollinger, Luke G. Showalter et.al., *UZ: A History of the United Zion Church, 1853-1980* (United Zion Church, 1981), pp. 9-14. John Miller, "The River Brethren," pp.20-22. Myron Dietz, "The Old Order River Brethren," *BICHL* (June 1983), 4-5. *ME*, Vol. V s.v., "Old Order River Brethren," by Stephen E. Scott. Ibid., "United Zion Church," by J. Paul Martin.

[128]Brechbill, *History Old Order River Brethren*, p. 38.

[129]Ibid., pp. 34-38. Personal interview with Myron Dietz, April 21, 1993. Stephen E. Scott, "Old Order River Brethren," *PMH* (July 1978), 13-15. John Miller, "The River Brethren," pp. 17-22. Eshleman, "River Brethren Denominations," pp. 179. 190.

[130]Scott, "Old Order River Brethren," *PMH*, 13-15. Personal interview with Myron Dietz, January 17, 1989.

[131]"Brief History of the Brethren in Christ," *Minutes of General Conference 1871-1904*, (Harrisburg, Pa.: Brethren in Christ Church, 1904), p. 314. Alderfer, "Mind of the Brethren," p. 96. Peter Brock, *Pacifism in the United States* (Princeton, N.J.: Princeton University Press, 1968), pp. 780-783. Brock indicates that in 1862 conscription was administered by the states. The federal draft act passed March 3, 1863. It is very likely that the Brethren in Christ sought federal recognition as a nonresistant body as a result of this act.

[132][Christian Lesher], "April 8, 1844," trans. Noah G. Good, p.1 (German photocopy of the original and an English translation in the Brethren in Christ Historical Library and Archives, Messiah College, hereafter referred to as HLA). I discovered the Christian Lesher papers at the Kittochtinny Historical Society Museum in Chambersburg, Pennsylvania, in March 1965 while engaged in research for my doctoral dissertation. I photocopied those papers that appeared relevant for my dissertation, thus I did not include all the papers. The March 16, 1965, issue of the Chambersburg daily newspaper, *Public Opinion*, reported the photocopying. Upon returning to the museum in 1987 for work on Christian Lesher, I was informed that the papers had been misplaced.

[133]Sider, *The Brethren in Christ in Canada*, pp. 50-55. Sider indicates that the name Tunker came from the German verb *"tunken,"* meaning to dip, and very likely applied to the Brethren because the Brethren baptized by immersion. Variations of the name as found in records are River Brethren, Brethren, Dunkers, Dunkarts, and Tunkerts. The name Tunker was used into the 1930s.

[134]The 1850 federal census record indicates that there were two John Hesses living in Franklin County, Washington Township, Pennsylvania, the township in which Christian Lesher lived. There is no way to verify which of the two, if either, is the John Hess mentioned, but it probably was one of the two mentioned. Letter of Roger B. Meyers to the author, May 17, 1992.

[135]"April 21, 1851," trans. Noah Good, single sheet. German photocopy of the original and English translation in HLA. Daniel Engle was a bishop in the Dauphin-Lebanon District, a son of Jacob Engel, the first Brethren in Christ leader. Daniel was an influential leader among the Brethren in Christ at the mid-nineteenth century. It has been reported (oral tradition) that he would "saddle a horse and make tours to

Ohio encouraging the saints and warning sinners to repent." Brechbill, *History of the Old Order River Brethren*, p.23. Morris M. Engle, *History of the Engle family in America* (Mt. Joy, Pa.: The Bulletin Press, n.d.), pp. 102-103. Climenhaga, *History of the Brethren in Christ Church*, p. 75. *The Biographical Annals of Lebanon County* (Chicago: J.H. Beers, 1904), p. 513. The *Annals* characterized Engel as "one of the fine men of his time, upright and righteous . . ." and was "long one of the leading bishops" of the Brethren in Christ Church.

[136]"April 21, 1851."

[137]Letter of Christian Lesher to Jacob Riefer, June 2, 1851. Photocopy of the German original and English translation by Noah Good in the HLA. The 1850 United States Census lists five Riefers, one of which was a Jacob Riefer who lived either in the town of Lebanon or in Lebanon Township, Lancaster County. This Jacob Riefer could have been the person to whom the letter was sent. Brethren in Christ were living in Lebanon County at the time. More research is needed to determine if this Jacob Riefer was the Jacob Riefer of the letter. Letter of R. Meyers to the author, May 17, 1992.

[138]Micha Myer (1796-1866), son of Henry Meyer, is buried in the New Guilford Cemetery, Franklin County. Personal interview with Roger B. Meyer, January 21, 1992. Seilhammer, *Biographical Annals of Franklin County*, p. 377.

[139]No information has been found regarding Staub.

[140]The United States 1850 Census lists a Daniel Singer living in Washington Township, Franklin County. More research needs to be done to fully verify that the person in the census was the Daniel Senger of the Lesher letter. Letter of R. Meyers to the author, May 17, 1992. Christian Hoover (1793-1867), son of Henrich and Marie (Wenger) Hoover, spent most of his days living near Pleasant Hill in Franklin County. He was chosen as bishop about 1834 and was the leader of the Hooverites (named after him). He is buried in the Burkholder Cemetery located within the Letterkenny Army Depot. *ME*, Vol. V, s.v., "Christian Hoover," by Stephen E. Scott. Barbara H. Burkholder and Anna Mary Burkholder, *The Genealogy of Henrich Huber* (Pleasant Hill, Pa.: 1965), p. 60.

[141]Jacob Strickler, Jr. (1788-1859) was the bishop in York County and the leader of the movement that withdrew from the main body and became the Old Order River Brethren. The date of his conversion and the time of his being chosen as bishop are not known. No information beyond the information available from River Brethren history was found regarding Flory. A John Flory is mentioned in a letter sent from the Lancaster County Brethren to those in York County. The letter implies that Flory was a leader among the Old Order River Brethren. Brechbill, *History of the Old Order River Brethren*, pp. 36, 79. *ME*, Vol V, s.v., "Jacob Strickler Jr.," by Stephen E. Scott. Wittlinger, *Quest for Piety and Obedience*, p. 134.

[142]Plum may have been Michael Plum (1802-1881) of Franklin County. He is mentioned in the 1880 Directory of the Brethren in Christ Church. One source lists him as a bishop. He is buried in the Montgomery Brethren in Christ cemetery. Letter of R. Meyers to author, March 15, 1992. Letter of Avery Zook to author, June 24, 1992.

[143]The letter in English translation is in John Miller, "The River Brethren," 21-22. A copy of the German original is in Scott, "Old Order River Brethren," *PMH*, 15.

[144]Ibid. Hollinger, *UZ*, pp. 9-14. Willinger, *Quest for Piety and Obedience*, p. 134. David Stoner (1814-1881) became an Old Order River Brethren bishop. Brechbill, *History of the Old Order River Brethren*, pp. 82-84. Scott, "Old Order River Brethren," pp. 13-14.

[145]Letter of Christian Huber (Hoover) to friend dated February 10, 1857, trans. Samuel M. Bricker (spelling of the name is not clear). Copy of the letter from the Lancaster County Historical Society Library. I have seen two additional copies of the letter with smoother flowing English translation. Laban Brechbill indicated that the letter was sent to Franklin County Bishop Christian Oberholser who, according to Brechbill, was a brother-in-law to Christian Hoover. The two men were on opposite sides of the controversy. The letter is considered authentic because of the names mentioned, locations given, the piety manifested, and the mood of the letter. An effort should be made to find the original letter. Brechbill, *History of the Old Order River Brethren*, pp. 157-158.

[146]Chastised refers to what has been called the lesser ban or partial avoidance. Not all religious groups defined the punishment in the same way. Here apparently members in good standing were not to greet the guilty with the holy kiss, and the guilty were not to take part in communion and feetwashing. Personal interview with Myron Dietz, February 22, 1993. How this punishment was applied to a bishop is not known.

[147]No information was found regarding John Schenck.

[148]"November 17, 1853," trans. Noah Good, single sheet, Christian Lesher Papers. Photocopy of the German original and the English translation in HLA.

[149]Ira D. Landis, "The Origin of the Brethren in Christ and Its Later Divisions," *MQR* (October 1960), 304. Letter of Jacob and Ada Sollenberger to the author, July 14, 1989.

[150]Hoover letter. Brechbill, *History of the Old Order River Brethren*, pp. 35-123.

[151]Ibid.

[152]John Miller, "River Brethren," 20-22. Scott, "Old Order River Brethren," *PMH*, 13-16.

[153]Letter of Jacob and Ada Sollenberger to the author, July 14, 1989.

[154]John Miller, "River Brethren," 22. Scott, "Old Order River Brethren," *PMH*, 13-14. Wittlinger, *Quest for Piety and Obedience*, p. 134. Personal interview with Myron Dietz, April 21, 1993.

[155]Hoover letter. Short note, no title, trans. Noah Good, Christian Lesher papers, HLA. Jacob L. Sollenberger, "Division of the River Brethren in Mid-1880's," single sheet, copy received from the author. Sollenberger gained his information from J. Lester Myers (1892-1961) of the Montgomery Brethren in Christ Church; Myers, in turn, obtained the data from his grandfather, Jacob G. Lesher, a great-grandson of Bishop Christian Lesher.

[156]Hoover letter.

[157]Short note, no title, trans. Noah Good. In Christian Lesher papers, HLA.

[158]Hoover letter.

[159]David Stoner, letter dated March 27, 1856 from Hellam Township, York County. Two copies of the letter are located in HLA. One of the copies indicates that it was translated by Charles Baker, Stayner, Ontario, Canada (January 20, 1926).

The second copy is in a typed format and indicates that David Stoner wrote the letter. This second copy also contains the "Reply from Lancaster County to York Brethren."

[160]Letter of Avery Zook to author, June 13, 1994.

[161]Letter of L.T. Brechbill to author, September 2, 1970. Photocopy of the Bible page was sent to the author by Jacob and Ada Sollenberger.

[162]FCCH, RRO, FCDB, No. 19, p. 395.

[163]"News Notes," *The Village Record* (Waynesboro), September 11, 1856.

[164]Robinson and Strite, p. 657.

[165]RCCH, RRO, FCDB, No. 40, pp. 380-381.

APPENDIX A

Appendix A consists of the inventories of Henry Sr. and Mary Lesher. They give some insight into the lives of the couple. Someone with expertise in Pennsylvania rural life in colonial times could throw light on the life of the Leshers by using these inventories. Unfortunately, no inventories were found for Henry Jr. and Frena Lesher or for Christian and Catherine Lesher. The original spelling is retained.

INVENTORY OF HENRY LESHER
OF RAPHO TOWNSHIP, DECEASED
March 31, 1784

A true Inventory of all the Goods, Rights, Chattles and Credits which were of Henry Lesher late of Rapho Township, deceased.

	pound	shilling	pence
to his Cloaths	3	10	6
to a Shirt and Box		2	6
to a peper Mill		4	6
to 4 sickles 2 wetstones		1	6
to a Quart Bottle and a Tin vessel		2	3
to 2 bottles		2	
to a great Augar		2	6
to a Glass Mug		2	6
to a Pewter Bottle & wooden Mug		2	
to 2 drawing Knives		2	6
to 3 Augars		1	6
to 4 chissels		5	
to 1 Augars		2	
to tool to Sharpen the schythe		3	
to 2 Saws		5	
to a steel-yard		10	
to a Tonge and Chain		1	
to a Steel-yard and Rasp		7	6
to two Saws		5	

to some Pails and Buckets		5	
to some Joiner Tools		6	
to two Rings of a Beetle & an Ax		6	
to two Axes and two Wedges		8	6
to Sandhorns & a Pair of Cissars for Wool		4	
to Sole and upper Leather		1	6
to 2 Tonges & a Fire Shovel		2	6
to 5 Hows & 2 Shovels		8	6
to a Hetchel		7	6
to a ditto		7	6
Total	9	7	9
to an Oil-pot and Wood Card		1	6
to a Fire Tonge		1	6
to 3 Iron Spoons and Fork		3	6
to two Tin Mugs and a Knife		1	6
to 7 Pewter Spoons & a Funnel		2	9
to 2 Kithin Panns		5	
to 4 dishes and some Plates		5	
to a small Pan and Hatchet		1	6
to a Pan and a Bleathing Tool		7	6
to a Pewter Plate		1	6
to 5 buckets		3	
to a Pewter Plate		2	6
to two Iron Potts		3	
to a copper Kettle		7	6
to a Meal (?) Box		10	
to a Skin and two sieves, Seven Baggs		12	
to a Hay Fork		1	6
to Books		6	9
to a Spectule		5	
to a Bleeding Instrument		9	
to two Iron Wedges		2	6
to a House Clock with the Box	1	5	
to a Stove with 5 plates		15	
to a black cow	3		
to 2 Tubs & Dung Forks		7	
to a Table		12	6

to a Weaving Loom with its Tools	2	10	
to two Sheep		18	
to a Straw Bench		4	6
to a Hand Bible		2	6
to an Iron			6
to Pennsylvania Paper Money	8	2	6
to Maryland Paper Money	16	2	6
to Passable Money Bond	140		
to Graint Stone		8	6

We the Subscribers testify, that in the above Praisement, we have acted Sincerely and to the best of our knowledge

his
Steven Wenger
mark
Henry Hackman

INVENTORY OF MARY LESHER, DECEASED
October the 20th, 1784

Inventory of the Goods and Chattels of Mary Lesher late Deceased taken and appraised by us the Subscribers the same being as follows viz:

	pound	shilling	pence
to 2 Jackets 2 Lineey Petecoats		7	6
to 9 Shifts		16	
to a Small Baskt with Caps and hankerchefs		2	
to 9 yards of Tow Linnin		9	
to 18 ½ yards of Linsey full'd	2	6	
to 4 yards Two Linnin		4	
to a beed Tick		5	
to 3 yards of blu Linsey		6	
to 2 yards of Brown Linsey		4	

to 4 yards of flax Linnin		8	
to 1 ½ yards of flax Linnin		3	
to 2 yards of tow Linnin		3	
to 3 ½ yards half tow Linnin		5	
to 1 ½ yards of Cloth		2	6
to 2 pillow Cases		5	
to 1 tow Sheet		3	
to 3 tow Sheets		7	6
to 4 pillow Cases		6	
to 1 Beed Tick		5	
to 2 Sheets		2	6
to 2 Beed Ticks		5	
to 2 Flax Tabel Clothes		6	
to 6 Towels		4	
to 2 pair of Stockings		2	
to Some flax		1	6
to 9 yards of flax tow Linnin		12	
to Stocking yarn		1	6
to 23 ? of Linnin yarn	1	5	
to 2 Boxes with Sundrys		1	6
to 1 Box			6
to 2 ? of wax		2	
to 1 ½ yard tow Linnin		2	
to 9 Spones		2	
to a Bag with Sundrys		1	
to 1 Bag Chaff		1	
to a Bag with Hatz		4	
to a Bag with Musterd			6
to a pair Skales		5	
to 1 Peper Mill		2	
to kives and forks		1	6
to 1 old Coat		1	
to 1 old blanket			6
to 1 Bag with yarn		1	
to 2 ash Cloths		2	
to 1 Small Bag with Wollen yarn and a pair Shears		1	6
to 3 Jackcoats		5	

to 3 pair of Trousers		1	
to 6 Shirts		12	
to Baskets		2	
to a Clock		10	
to a Beed	1	10	
to 2 Hackels		15	
to a paire of pinchers and old Iron		1	
to 7 Baskets		1	
to 2 Lamps			9
to 3 Baskets		1	
to 1 vinegar Cask			6
to 1 Cask		1	6
to 1 Drawing Knife & Butcher knife		1	
to Sundry Glasses		2	
to 10 Bottels		6	
to 2 horse Shoes and Shakel			6
to Sundrys old Truk			6
to 2 Bags		2	
to 1 Bag with Bran		2	
to Rye and Indian corn		2	
to 2 Bags with Dry apels		6	
to 1 Butter Tub		9	
to 2 Shaws and Leder		3	
to a Basket and Reel			6
to 4 Pans		5	
to 2 Sinning weels		5	
to 1 watering pot a bag with flax seed		4	
to 1 Dung fork 2 Shebels a Dunk Hock			3
to 2 axes and a foot ax		6	
to 1 Coper Kettel		4	
to 1 Iron pot and Kettel		2	
to 1 flax Brake		2	
to a Small Saw & Hammer		1	
to flax		7	6
to 2 Hows 2 Beehives		1	6
to a Basket a paire of Shears		1	6
to Sundry wooden vesels		4	
to Sundry Ceder vesels		2	

to 2 Butter Dishes 4 plates & a platter		8	
to 1 Iron Ladel and flesh fork		2	
to Pin Hare		1	
to an Iron Stove		15	
to 1 Paire of Trousers			2
to a paire of Coopers Tongs			6
to 1 Cow with a Bell	2	10	
to 2 Booking Tubs & Pickel Tub		5	
to first and Second Crops of Hay	1	5	
to Indian Corn and Some Bakon		1	
to 1 Stool			9
to Cash in hard Money		9	
to 6 aprons		5	
to 20 Books	1	5	
to Weaver Spool		1	
to a Paire of Women pockets		2	
to 6 Tabel Cloths		15	
	28	4	2
to one Beed	1		
to 3 Sheep	1	8	
	30	12	2

This inventory was Taken and the Good therein Mentioned appraised by us the Subscribers this 20th of Oct. 1784

his
Steven Wenger
mark
John Hagey

Exhibited into the Register's Office at Lancaster the 1st. Day of November Anno Domiri 1784.

his
John Lesher Adm.
mark

APPENDIX B

On the inner side of the back cover of Christian Lesher's Sauer Bible is a listing of the death and life span of sixteen persons all related to the Christian Lesher family. The text indicates that Christian Lesher was the recorder until his own death was inscribed. Below is a photocopy of the German original, an English translation of the same, and a limited identification of some members. Noah Good was the translator; Lesher genealogist James Lesher provided the identification information.

English Translation	Identification
Jacob Lesher died on August 29, 1796 at age 30 years and 6 months	Brother of Christian Lesher, did not marry
Mother died on July 6, 1804 age, 60 years	Christian Lesher's mother, maiden name, Frena Zette
Father died November 7, 1821 age 81 years, 3 months, 7 days	Christian Lesher's father, Henry Lesher, Jr.
My brother Heinrich died December 18, 1828 age 56 years, 8 months	Christian's brother, married Maria Longenecker
My sister Maria died January 24, 1838 age 69 years, 5 days	Christian's sister, married Jacob Stoner
My sister Fronica died April 7, 1841, age 70 years, 11 months	"Fanny," Christian's sister married Jacob Wengard
Jacob Wenger died February 12, 1842, age 70 years, 4 months	no data
Jacob Steiner died December 11, 1844, age 73 years, 2 months	no data
Heinrich Lescher's wife died Dec. 7, 1845, age 79 years, 9 months	Her husband's death (Heinrich Lescher) noted above. Her maiden name, Maria Longenecker

Christian Lescher died September 6, 1856, age 81 years, 4 months & 11 days	The Christian Lesher of the article
Catharine Lescher died February 15, 1865, age 85 years, 5 months, 25 days	The Catherine (Streit) Lesher of this article
Maria Sarwer died February 22, 1864, age 85 years, 9 months, 11 days	Sister of Catherine (Streit); married John Sarver
Magdalena, Streit died April 18, 1864, age 83 years, 1 month, 14 days	Second sister of Catharine Lescher, did not marry
Polly Lescher died April 7, 1864, age 58 years, 14 days	no data
Maria Lesher died November 16, 1866, age 58 years, 11 months, 7 days	no data
Jacob Miller died February 28, 1877, age 63 years, 4 months, 13 days	Cousin of Christian Lescher

Christian Lesher's Library

Significant insight into Christian Lesher's views can be gained by an examination of his books. The little evidence available suggests that his formal education was very limited, which is not surprising, given that the Pennsylvania public school system developed following his youth. Lesher "home-schooled" himself in the fields of theology and spirituality. He read and wrote in his inherited German language.

Fortunately, in the mid-1950s, Lesher's library was donated by Daniel G. H. Lesher (a descendant) to the Kittochtinny Historical Library and Museum in Chambersburg, Pennsylvania. Some of the books in this collection were published after Lesher's death, thus could not have been used by Lesher. Others, however, can be identified as Lesher's books, either by his signature or the known use he made of them.

Lesher inscribed his name in three books authored by Johann Arndt (1555-1621). Arndt, a Lutheran pastor in Germany, was a forerunner of and foundational to the rise of German Pietism. Arndt's *True Christianity* (which Lesher bought in 1810, according to his note in the book), was widely read and translated into many languages (including some in Africa and Asia), and was influential in preparing the soil for an experience-oriented faith. Arndt emphasized heart-centered repentance, self-denial, sanctification, and a progressive inner intimacy with and an outer righteousness modeled on Christ.

Arndt was an able preacher. He sought to edify and strengthen the heart more than to theologize the head. True Christianity, he insisted, cannot be only an outward conformity to statements of doctrine and going through the sacraments; it must also be seen in changes in attitudes, affections, and lifestyle.[1]

A second important Pietist-oriented work in Lesher's library was Philip Jacob Spener's *Der Hochwichtige von der Wiedergeburt* (*The

Highly Significant Work of the New Birth), published in 1696. Lesher purchased the book in 1805 for the price of fifteen shillings, according to a note in the book. The volume contains sixty-six sermons by Spener (1635-1705). The piety enunciated in it is very similar to Arndt's. Both focused on personal spiritual renewal and a life lived in keeping with God's will.

Spener's small work, *Pia Desideria* (*Pious Desires*), originally an introduction to Arndt's *True Christianity*, was a clarion call for the revitalization of the Christian faith. In the first section, Spener is critical of the secular princes using the church for their political ends; he reprimands Lutheran clergy and theologians for their polemicism and sophistry; he rejects the view that baptism, confession, absolution, and the Lord's Supper are automatically efficacious; rather they undermine motivation for holy living. And he censures the common people for their drunkenness and low moral standards.   Such shallow Christianity, he maintains,   negates evangelistic efforts among Jews, Roman Catholics, and heretics.[2]

In the last section of *Pious Desires*, Spener outlines a program for the renewal of the church. It includes small group meetings to foster Christian growth, all Christians acting as priests (the priesthood of believers) in offering their bodies as sacrifices to God, engaging in prayer and meditation, converting sinners, and comforting the weak.[3]

Although Spener was critical of the spiritual condition of the Lutheran Church in Germany, he insisted on reform from within the church through transformed hearts, holy living, and caring relations. He did not reject infant baptism, but he taught the need for a new heart. He called for more church discipline, yet realized that this would not be effective without a new inner attitude. The new heart was important, not correct outer form and mental assent to rationalistic doctrine.

Spener's *Pious Desires*, along with his other writings and his churchmanship, launched German Pietism. The term, initially one of derision coined by opponents of the movement, came into use during the time of Spener's ministry. *Pious Desires* evoked a strong, positive response in the Lutheran Church and elsewhere. At the same time, it was strongly opposed by those with the rationalistic theology identified as Protestant Orthodoxy. After the death of

Luther, Lutheran theologians gave themselves to a rational systematizing of doctrine; in this work they were influenced by natural theology and Aristotelian logic. They engaged in "fine-tuning" and "hair-splitting" of theology, often becoming polemical and argumentative as they sought to undercut each other. Generally they were insensitive to ethical issues. The result was spiritual and moral lethargy. Spener's thought and writing were in reaction to these conditions.

An important innovation of Spener as a pastor was small private groups known as *collegia pietatis* (gatherings for piety)—or conventicles, as they were frequently called. These small groups met for spiritual renewal through prayer, Bible study, discussion of sermons, and reading devotional materials—all to aid one another in spiritual growth. Some were led by pastors, others by lay leaders; some met in homes, others in churches. They supplemented, not supplanted, the state-established church.[4]

It was such small group meetings that played a role in the rise of the Brethren in Christ. Mennonite Martin Boehm (later a United Brethren in Christ leader), invigorated by the Pietist currents in Lancaster County, Pennsylvania, became something of an itinerant evangelist, holding meetings and forming small, informal groups similar to the European conventicles. Three of these—at Pequea (Pequea Brethren), at Conestoga (Conestoga Brethren), and one by the Susquehanna River (River Brethren) after a time parted from Martin Boehm and bonded together around 1780 to become the River Brethren.[5]

Although none of the writings of August Hermann Francke (1663-1727) are in Lesher's library, Francke was second only to Spener in influencing the rise, spread, and organization of the Pietist movement. Influenced by Spener, Francke studied in four German universities; with Spener's aid he was appointed as a professor of Greek and oriental languages at the new University of Halle. Due to Francke's work, Halle became a Pietist citadel, promoting the new concept of a heart-felt faith and sending out energized disciples who spread the Pietist concept of the faith in northern Europe and overseas.

Francke was active in other ways. He was a pastor. He pioneered charitable institutions, including schools for both poor and rich children, an orphanage, and homes for the aged, widows, and handicapped people. He established a publishing house and a missionary center, placing Halle and Pietism in the forefront of the emerging Protestant missionary movement (two Halle graduates went to India in 1706). Pietism, with its emphasis on personal conversion, holy living, optimism about the Christian future, and its small conventicles created a dynamic foundation for the eighteenth- to twentieth-century world-wide missionary endeavor.

An important development in Pietism was Francke's vivid crisis conversion experience. At the beginning of his university studies, he was more entangled with worldly vanity than with a serious consideration of the faith. Although he studied theology, he aimed at becoming a distinguished scholar, rich in means and living a easy life. At the same time, beset by sins he became burdened in heart; the thought of denying Christ at times brought him to his knees in tears. His conversion came as he was troubled by the sermon he was to give the next day. "Then the Lord heard me," he wrote, "when I was still on my knees. So great was his fatherly love that . . . he suddenly heard me. . . . Then, as one turns his hand 'in a twinkling,' so all my doubts were gone; I was sure in my heart of the grace of God in Jesus Christ. . . . I was suddenly so overwhelmed with a stream of joy that I praised God out of high spirits. . . . I arose again of a completely different mind than when I had knelt down." This crisis experience would later become normative in conversion, especially in American public revivalism.[6]

Another book in Lesher's library was Gottfried Arnold's *Wahre Abbildung der ersten Christen nach ihrem Lebendigen Glauben und heligen Leben* (*A Faithful Portrayal of the First Christians According to Their Living and Saintly Lives*). A church historian, pietist, and later Lutheran pastor, Arnold (1666-1714) played a substantial role in shaping Radical Pietism. He was very critical of state-established churches (he called them "pharisaic institutions"), considering them as obstacles to true spirituality. Given his mystical-spiritualistic piety, he stressed the need for a crisis new birth experience ("repentance struggle"), mystical union with Christ, and a life lived in imitation of Christ-like love. He saw the early church as the ideal community, comprised only of regenerated believers whose lives were to be emulated by all Christians. He noted that often in the history of Christianity, those persecuted for being heretics were the most faithful witnesses to the truth, while the persecutors were the real heretics.

Later, Arnold moderated his views, became a Lutheran pastor, and married. Some radical pietists were disappointed when he married, more so when he fathered a child.[7] Arnold came to believe that the true church is invisible (membership in it is a matter of the heart). He moved away from his idea that Adam was androgynous (both male and female in one person) before the fall, and that the separation into two sexes and resultant human sexuality was a result of the fall.

Arnold's writings were well received by some of the smaller churches in southeastern Pennsylvania during colonial times. His views helped to shape the German Baptist Brethren in their European beginnings (1708), and later their belief in the centrality of an inner spiritual regeneration that issued in a life patterned after Jesus Christ. Equally important as an influence on the German Baptist Brethren was Arnold's belief in the normativeness of such practices in the primitive church as believers immersion baptism and the proper use of church discipline.[8] The founders of the United Brethren in Christ, especially Philip Otterbein and the Evangelical Association, were shaped in part by Arnold's emphasis on an experience-centered faith, patterning all of life by following the Christ within the heart, and fostering true spirituality through non-established and non-partisan fellowships.[9]

Mennonites also read Arnold. Children of the Anabaptists, the Mennonites, became quietistic and withdrawn, originally in large part because of persecution. Some of them were renewed through Pietism with its emphasis on personal conversion, the inner presence of Jesus, and the enriching of spirituality through Bible reading, devotions, and hymnody. To suggest that Arnold was a mediator between Anabaptism and Pietism is an overstatement, but he did commend the Mennonites for their "piety, godly living, brotherly love, simple obedience, steadfastness in persecution and defenselessness." At the same time, he criticized them for their "legalism . . . Pharisaism . . . and divisiveness."[10]

In summary, it is apparent that Arnold's writings were influential at the time of Brethren in Christ origin. It is understandable that Christian Lesher would relate to some of Arnold's views.

His library also included (without his signature, unlike most of his books) a copy of John Bunyan's *Pilgrim's Progress* in German translation.[11] Lesher makes reference to Bunyan in his writings.[12] The Puritans, among whom was Bunyan, were initially concerned with purifying the Church of England from its "popish" remnants. As their movement developed, they sought to create a "Holy Commonwealth," and emphasized the new heart and personal righteousness.[13] In the process, a pietistic Puritanism came into being that had no essential differences from continental Pietism.[14] It is instructive to note that in the early years of the official paper of the Brethren in Christ, the *Evangelical Visitor* (beginning date 1887), some articles expressed appreciation for *Pilgrim's Progress*. Writers of such articles recognized the relationship between German Pietism and other similar developments in Europe.[15]

Another work in Lesher's collection was the first hymnal published (1744) for the German Baptist Brethren in Colonial America. Entitled *Das Klaine davidische Psalterspiel der Kinder* (*The Small Davidic Psaltery of the Children of Zion*), most of its hymns were written by Pietists, and there is evidence that the work influenced the first known Brethren in Christ hymnal, *Geistlichen Liedern* (*Spiritual Hymns*), published in 1874.[16]

Also in Lesher's holdings were books in the Anabaptist tradition. One was T. J. van Braght's *Der blutige Schau-Platz oder Martyrer-Spiegel der tauffs Gesinnten oder wehrlosen Christen* (*The Bloody Theater of Martyrs Mirror of the Defenseless Christians*). The first part consists of martyr accounts covering the first fifteen centuries of Christianity; the second part describes the Anabaptist martyrs of the sixteenth century. When war threatened in Colonial America, Pennsylvania Mennonites, in order to emphasize nonresistance, had the *Mirror* translated from the Dutch language into German and printed at the Ephrata Cloisters (1748-1751).[17] An early copy of the *Mirror* in the Brethren in Christ Historical Library and Archives indicates that some Brethren in Christ were acquainted with the work.

Another book of Anabaptist origins in Lesher's library was the oldest Anabaptist hymnbook, the *Ausbund*. Its first songs were written (1535-1540) by Anabaptists in prison; by 1564 they were collected into book form. The lyrics emphasized suffering, the cross, martyrdom, and the wickedness of the relentless world; at the same time they expressed a hopefulness in tribulation, confidence in God's triumph, and the glory of heaven. Other prominent themes were believers baptism and nonresistance. The first American edition of the *Ausbund* was printed in 1742 and was used by Pennsylvania Mennonites well into the eighteenth century. Increasingly, pietist-oriented songs were included in newer Mennonite hymnals.[18]

Lesher used Menno Simon's *Buchvon der Taufe (Book on Baptism)* to state the case for believers baptism. However his library does not contain the book.

Lesher's use of both Pietist and Anabaptist sources indicates that he was in the tradition of the founders of the Brethren in Christ in bringing together elements of the two movements. His purchase of Pietist sources (some radical) in his early, formative years and his use of Pietist language and ideas suggest that he was strongly influenced by Pietism. (It may be of some significance that he wrote his name in and the price he paid for each of the Pietist books, but not for those of Anabaptist orientation.) In being attracted to both Pietism and Anabaptism, Lesher (like other early Brethren in Christ) was similar to the German Baptist Brethren.[19] Some Mennonite historians-theologians have seen the impact of Pietism on their group in a negative light. But it seems increasingly clear that some of the descendants of the Anabaptists were invigorated by Pietism in a number of ways.[20]

Lesher had access to a German translation of Charles Buck's *Theological Dictionary*. Buck (1771-1815) was an English dissenter clergyman. His dictionary, widely used and reprinted numerous times, was evangelical in orientation and sympathetic toward the Wesleyan movement (although his writings also reflect some Calvinistic ideas).[21]

While he wrote in the German language, Lesher was interested in speaking and writing in English, as shown by a book he bought in 1810. As indicated by its English title, *A Useful Book to Aid and*

Teach Germans to Speak English, the book was explicitly written to help German-speaking people to learn English.[22]

In his study of the Bible, Lesher used four versions/translations: Martin Luther's, Sauer's, Froschauer's, and the Berleburg. Luther's translation had the status among German-speaking people that the King James version had in the English world. It was widely used in Pennsylvania.

J. Christoph Sauer (1695-1758), although not a member of the German Baptist Brethren, was in sympathy with their values.[23] At the printing business that he founded in Germantown, he published in 1743 the first so-called Sauer Bible. His son, Christopher Sauer II (1721-1784), unlike his father a member and leader of the German Baptist Brethren, published the second and third editions of the Sauer Bible. Lesher owned a copy of the third (printed in 1776).

Using Luther's translation with some Pietist editing, Sauer I affixed an appendix consisting of Esdras 3 and 4 and Maccabees 3 of the Old Testament Apocrypha, using the Berleburg Bible version of these two books.[24] Colonial German Reformed and Lutheran clergy (e.g., Henry M. Muhlenberg) were very critical of the Sauer Bible, including among their objections the appendix from the Apocrypha and the use of the Berleburg translation. On the whole, believers church groups, such as the German Baptist Brethren and the Mennonites, preferred the Sauer Bibles.[25]

An examination of Lesher's Sauer Bible shows that it was one of his personal, or working, Bibles. It printed parallel or related Scripture verses immediately below some of the Scripture verses. To these Lesher added additional citations, a practice that related well to his tendency to add verse after verse in his writings.

The Froschauer Bible came out of the Zwinglian Reformation headed by Swiss Reformer Ulrich Zwingli (1484-1531) in Zurich, Switzerland. The first Zurich Bibles (New Testament in 1524, entire Bible in 1529) were printed by the well-known Zurich publisher, Christian Froschauer, and were based on Luther's translation with some alterations in word order, vocabulary, and vocalization to fit the Swiss setting. The new translation was well received: the type was clear, the pictorial drawings attractive, and the language popular. Especially the Swiss Anabaptists were fond of it.[26]

Luther was slow in translating the books of the Old Testament prophets, with the result that Froschauer substituted translations by Ludwig Haetzer, who had some Anabaptist tendencies, and Hans Denck, an Anabaptist who emphasized the work of the Holy Spirit. The translations by Haetzer and Denck were not accepted by the state church clergy; in contrast, Swiss Anabaptists favored the first edition of the Froschauer Bible, so much so that it came to be identified as the Anabaptist Bible and its reprinting in the Bern canton forbidden (authorities confiscated copies when they found them).[27]

The Anabaptist preference for the Froschauer Bible led to Pennsylvania Mennonites having the New Testament reprinted in 1787.[28] This positive attitude toward the Froschauer translation continues to the present among some Anabaptist descendants. It was reprinted in 1975, and is used at certain times by the Hutterites and the Amish.[29]

Lesher brought his copy of the Froschauer Bible (printed in 1538 in Zurich) to Franklin County when he moved there from Lancaster County.[30] As will be noted, he used it in his writings. Two copies of the Froschauer Bible in the Brethren in Christ Archives is further evidence that it was used by other early Brethren in Christ leaders.

It comes as a surprise that Lesher used the Berleburg Bible. To date no evidence has been found that other Brethren in Christ used it. Lesher bought his copy in 1819 for $30.[31]

The Bible gained its name from the small town of Berleburg in the principality of Wittgenstein, Germany (today it is in the state of North Rhine-Westphalia in the west-central part of Germany). In the seventeenth and eighteenth centuries, Wittgenstein was divided into two smaller principalities (government subdivisions): Sayn-Wittgenstein-Hohenstein and Sayn-Wittgenstein-Berleburg. The village of Schwarzenau, the place of German Baptist Brethren origins (1708), was in the former principality, the town of Berleburg in the latter. Wittgenstein was ruled by Count Johann Casimer (1687-1741) when the Bible was published. Because he was sympathetic to Pietists, radical Pietists who became the German Baptist Brethren, found refuge in his territory, as did those radicals who published the Berleburg Bible.[32]

Given the close proximity of Schawarzenau to Berleburg and that radical Pietists lived in both places, German Baptist and other scholars have tried to determine if the Schwarzenau group (German Baptist Brethren) was involved in publishing the Berleburg Bible. According to one source, the elder Alexander Mack assisted financially. Although some scholars claim that the German Baptist Brethren played an important role, the weight of the evidence suggests that they were interested in the project but did not formally join in the work.

The evidence for this is threefold. First, the Schwarzenau Brethren were largely craftsmen, not trained scholars knowledgeable of biblical languages. Second, the Brethren were not on amicable terms with Johann Haug, the chief Berleburg Bible editor. Third, some of the Brethren left Wittgenstein for Pennsylvania before the first volume was published; almost all of them were in Penn's colony by 1729, thirteen years before the last volume came off the press. However, they were sympathetic to the project and to an extent used the Berleburg Bible.[33]

The Berleburg Bible was in process of publication from 1726-1742.[34] Printed in eight folio volumes and bound in four books, the Bible contained 6,201 pages. The commentary and interpretations to the biblical text (four times as long as the text) give the Bible its significance. The Berleburg Bible included (following Revelation) the Old Testament Apocrypha, some Old Testament Pseudepigraphal works, a few New Testament Apocryphal titles, and some of the writings of the Apostolic Fathers. The biblical text, a revision of Luther's work, was translated from the original Hebrew and Greek with great care because the translators believed that at times the hidden meaning of the text was in the accents and nuances of the original biblical languages.[35]

The enlarged canon in the Berleburg Bible was based on the belief that the decisions of the early church in determining the canon were not infallible. The translators considered that the early church fathers were too much tied to tradition-bound outer practices and blinded by rationalistic theology. The fall of the church, they maintained, began with the creedal Greek-oriented Trinitarian formulations of the early church.[36] Those who produced the Berleburg Bible thought themselves to be informed by heart spirituality, as were the original writers of the Bible. Thus the

Berleburg translators and editors maintained that they could re-open the canon.

Several levels were discerned in their approach to Scripture: literal, moral, spiritual, and the hidden/secret. The literal referred, as noted above, to a very careful translation from the Hebrew and Greek in order to perceive the distinctive colorations of the original languages. With the literal came the spiritually directed moral element: the serious mind of the devout will give full attention to ethical considerations. Finally, the hidden/secret experience or communion is in the soul: repentance, purification, illumination, and, at last, mystical unification with God. It is the Spirit that moves people to the true inner life beyond the words and accounts recorded in Scripture. The gaining of mystical union was helped by allegorical, typological, and numerological interpretations of the text.[37]

The commentary of the Berleburg Bible was scholarly, although not in its theological precision or its scholarly sophistication; rather, it was in the research done and in the use of much of the western evangelical heritage. Use was made of Latin, German, English, Dutch, and French reference works, as well as the Bible commentaries in those languages. A vast number of scholars and authors are cited and quoted—ancient philosophers, Jewish authorities, early church fathers, medieval theologians, Protestant exegetes, Renaissance humanists, and heart-warmed Pietists. The editors explained the hidden meaning of the text; they were especially informed by quietists and mystics, such as Madame Guyon, Jane Leade, and Antoine Bourignon.[38]

The Berleburg Bible was individualistically-oriented, in relation both to the conversion experience and the ongoing experiential life. It was the heart that gave shape to the moral life and contour to the nature of group associations. The universal church was an invisible entity consisting of all who experience religion in a heart-felt way; such people possibly were in all churches. The Berleburg Bible distinguished the invisible church of the Spirit (the *true* church) from the visible church (the church of outer appearance). Such an understanding explains how the true church may be seen to transcend rationalistic, confessing, organizational structures, as well as national boundaries.

At the same time, the Berleburg Bible had a place for the local body consisting of the converted, of those voluntarily drawn together to be a holy fellowship. Such a group could enhance spirituality for individual members.

The Berleburg Bible held that true baptism was not the outer baptism but inner assurance, cleansing, and union with God. In a similar vein, communion (the Lord's Supper) centered on an inner union with Christ. Reference is made to church discipline, but in practice the users of the Berleburg Bible moved away from the formation of disciplined communities; direction was found by the local society as individual hearts came to a common mind.[39]

In the religious fervor of Colonial America, various groups embraced a heart-centered belief. In Pennsylvania, pro-Pietist German clergy from the established churches in Europe (Lutheran and Reformed) sought to indigenize Pietism within the parameters of their traditions.[40] Such bodies did not accept the Berleburg Bible. But it was treasured by such radical Pietists as Conrad Beissel and the Ephrata commune, and by such spiritualists as some of the Schwenkfelders. The spirituality fostered by the Berleburg Bible also had some influence among the United Brethren in Christ and the Evangelical Association.[41]

Copies of the Berleburg Bible could be bought in the colonies by 1746. Christoph Sauer I was an agent for its sale. The extent to which German Baptist Brethren bought it cannot be fully determined, but it does appear that it was used by at least some of the group during the time that the Brethren spoke the German language.[42]

This history and explanation of the Berleburg Bible is not to suggest that Lesher was strongly influenced by that version. But he did use it in a discriminating manner.

The same awakening that brought the United Brethren in Christ into being also led to the origin of the Brethren in Christ. Among the already existing bodies in Pennsylvania, the German Baptist Brethren had more in common with those who were to found the River Brethren (later Brethren in Christ) around 1780. These founders first sought immersion baptism with the German Baptist Brethren, then immersion only. When problems arose regarding this request, the River Brethren organized themselves as a new body of believers.[43]

Because he resided in Franklin County, Pennsylvania, during his adult life, Lesher lived among German Baptist Brethren. That body had a meetinghouse (the Antietam Meetinghouse) one and a half miles north of Lesher's house. One mile north of this meetinghouse was the Snow Hill Community, a daughter commune of the Ephrata Cloisters. Snow Hill was not as rigidly ascetic as its parent and was more evangelical. Its members believed in the new birth, trine immersion, feetwashing, the holy kiss, nonresistance, and the love feast. Among other translations, they used the Berleburg Bible.[44]

As in his books, so in his Bibles Lesher was influenced by his Anabaptist roots and the more recent Pietist renewal. The Froschauer Bible came out of Swiss Anabaptism, the Sauer Bible was published in Colonial Pennsylvania, the Berleburg Bible issued from the ferment of radical Pietism. The Berleburg Bible commentary had some influence in shaping his Pietist sympathies. In his understanding of personal, or heart, piety, he was Pietist; in his perception of corporate piety, he identified with the group life of Anabaptism. In his writings, Lesher called for a heart-changing conversion, a commitment to evangelism, a life of holy living modeled after Jesus Christ, and a brotherhood patterned after the New Testament church.

Although limited in formal education and belonging to a body not given to professional theological education or discussion, Christian Lesher brought together a library of surprising scope.

NOTES

[1] *True Christianity* was published in Nurnberg, Germany in 1762. A copy is in the Historical Library and Archives (Brethren in Christ Church) at Messiah College (hereafter referred to as HLA). This work was widely read in Pennsylvania Dutch country both during and after colonial times, including by Lutheran, Reformed, German Baptist, Brethren, Moravians, Mennonites, Schwendkfelders, and the Ephrata Community. Eli Engle (1857-1949), a great-grandson of Jacob Engel, owned a copy. For Arndt, see F. Ernest Stoeffler, *The Rise of Evangelical Pietism* (Leiden, Netherlands: E.J. Brill, 1965), pp. 202-212. A recent translation of *True Christianity* was published in 1979 by the Paulist Press (New York), Peter C. Erb translator; Erb in his "Introduction" (pp. 1-17) and Heiko A. Oberman in the "Preface" (pp. Xi-xvii) ably introduce Arndt. See also *Westminster Dictionary of the Christian Church*, s.v. "Arndt, Johann," and Roger E. Olson, *The Story of Christian Theology* (Downers Grove: InterVarsity Press, 1999), pp. 477-479.

[2]Spener, *Pia Desideria*, pp. 39-75. See Dale R. Stoffer, *Background and Development of Brethren Doctrines 1650-1987* (Philadelphia: Brethren Encyclopedia, 1989), p. 14. See also Stoeffler, *Evangelical Pietism*, pp. 232, 233.

[3]For a summary of the last section of *Pious Desires*, see Peter C. Erb, ed. and trans., "Introduction," in *Pietists: Selected Writings* (N.Y.: Paulist Press, 1983), pp. 5-6. Also see Manfred W. Kohl, "Spener's Pia Desideria—The Programmschrift of Pietism," in *Contemporary Perspectives on Pietism* (Chicago, Ill.: Covenant Press, February-May, 1976), pp. 61-78.

[4]K. James Stein, *Philipp Jakob Spener: Pietist Patriarch* (Chicago: Covenant Press, 1986), pp. 19-24, 57-127. Stein summarizes the impact of *Pia Desideria*: "Its moral earnestness, tightly honed arguments, appeal to the inner life of each person (instead of reform by disciplinary means), and its balanced judgments gave the book a ready hearing. Spener was cognizant of the limitations of the Church's temporal existence, but would not surrender to them. He believed that, in the power of God, the Church might become something more." That is to say, Spener saw the weaknesses of a state church, but he concluded the answer was a renewal movement within the state church. Pietism was strongly opposed by Protestant Orthodoxy. See Olson, *The Story of Christian Theology*, pp. 473-481.

[5]Owen H. Alderfer, "The Mind of the Brethren in Christ: A Synthesis of Revivalism and the Church Conceived as Total Community" (Ph.D. diss., Claremont Graduate School and University Center, 1964).

[6]Gary R. Sattler, *God's Glory, Neighbor's Good: A Brief Introduction to the Life and Times of August Herman Francke* (Chicago, Ill.: Covenant Press, 1982), pp. 25-35, 46-67, 77-88. See also Ted A. Campbell, *The Religion of the Heart: A Study of European Religious Life in the Seventeenth and Eighteenth Centuries* (Columbia, S.C.: University of South Carolina Press, 1991), pp. 78-91.

Some historians have subdivided developments within German Pietism into church-state Pietism, radical Pietism, and believers church Pietism. Common to all three was an experiential revitalization of the Christian faith; the importance of personal heart renewal; the desire and ability (inspired by the Holy Spirit) to live a holy life; gathering into small groups (conventicles) for edification, instruction, and mutual encouragement, and a sense of compassion for the spiritual, moral, and physical well-being of others. Much devotional material and many songs of piety were written. Sermons became heart-searching and heart-warming. Occupation with outer form and rationalistic theology were seen as debilitating.

Church-state pietists (Lutheran, Reformed) sought to invigorate their communions through being a spiritual yeast and energizing dynamic from within their churches. They viewed the Protestant Reformation as effecting a biblical reforming of the Christian faith, but they thought that the vitality of the Reformation was ebbing, especially in the areas of inner motivation and sanctified living. They sometimes viewed the conventicles within the state churches as small churches within the church, thus infant baptism and the Lord's Supper were not part of conventicle activities.

Radical pietists, individualistic in outlook, separated themselves from state and believers churches. They emphasized the subjective/personal dimensions of the faith leading to a mystical union with God. They were more attuned to the guidance of the Holy Spirit than to the authority of the Word or words. Only inner prompting issued in outer actions. The sacraments were spiritualized. They understood the church to be invisible, encompassing all Christians. At the same time, small, informal groups, akin to conventicles, gathered and sharply separated themselves from state-established churches. They considered their corporate perfection to be actualized in the eternal kingdom of God, soon to be ushered in by God.

Believers church pietists rejected the belief that it was God's design that the church and state were to actualize the true Christian community, incorporating all citizens through infant baptism and maintaining orthodoxy by the power of the state. Rather, they emphasized that the church consists only of the converted, baptized, Christ-following, community-bonded disciples, empowered by the Spirit to reconstitute the New Testament fellowship of believers whose task was to carry out the Great Commission. The church anticipates God consummating history, and going beyond history, in the eternal kingdom of God. In that orientation, the present state was to maintain law and order and provide religious freedom, but it was not the co-director in establishing the kingdom of God.

See Stoeffler, *Evangelical Pietism*, pp. 9-23, and Stoeffler, *German Pietism During the Eighteenth Century* (Leiden, Netherlands: E.J. Brill, 1973), pp. 168-216; Donald F. Durnbaugh, *Brethren Beginnings* (Philadelphia: Brethren Encyclopedia, 1992), pp. 61-64; Dale Brown, *Anabaptism and Pietism* (Elizabethtown, Pa.: Young Center for the Study of Anabaptist and Pietist Groups, 1990), pp. 1-14; Stoffer, *Brethren Doctrines*, pp. 5-57; Martin H. Schrag, "The Impact of Pietism upon the Mennonites of Early American Christianity," in F. Ernest Stoeffler, ed., *Continental Pietism and Early American Christianity* (Grand Rapids, Mich.: William B. Eerdmans Publishing Company, 1976), pp. 74-122; Luke L. Keefer, Jr., "Three Streams in Our Heritage: Separate or Parts of a Whole?" *Brethren in Christ History and Life* (April 1996), 26-63.

[7]Stoffer, *Brethren Doctrines*, pp. 23-32; Peter C. Erb, "Introduction," in Erb, ed., *Pietists: Selected Writings*, pp. 13, 14.

[8]Gottfried Arnold, "Brethren Among Early Christians," *Brethren Life and Thought*, trans. and introd., Donald Miller (Summer 1957), 45, 45, 61; Alexander Mack, "A Brief and Single Exposition of the Outward Yet Sacred Rights and Ordinances of the House of God," in Donald F. Durnbaugh, comp. and trans., *European Origins of the Brethren* (Elgin, Ill.: The Brethren Press, 1986), p. 352.

[9]J. Steven O'Malley, *Early German-America Evangelicalism* (Lanham, Md.: The Scarecrow Press, 1995), pp. 3, 5, 171-74.

[10]Quoted from Stoffer, *Brethren Doctrines*, p. 57. See also Richard K. McMaster, *Land, Piety, Peoplehood* (Scottdale, Pa.: Herald Press, 1985), p. 57, see also pp. 47-56; Theron F. Schlabach, *Peace, Faith, Nation* (Scottdale, Pa.: Herald Press, 1988), pp. 88-95; *Mennonite Encyclopedia*, Vol. I, s.v. "Arnold, Gottfried," by Robert Friedmann. On early Pietism, Dale Brown has written: "Historically, Pietism emerged when much of the zeal had departed from the Anabaptist movement, flourishing best on Anabaptist soil and finding strength in such Anabaptist strongholds as Würtemberg. . . . Anabaptism and Pietism shared the same desire to carry the Reformation to its logical conclusion." Brown, *Understanding Pietism*, rev. ed. (Nappanee, Ind.: Evangel Press, 1996), p. 17.

[11]Published in Harrisburg, Pennsylvania in 1828 by Gustab C. Peters.

[12]See, for example, his "The Spiritual Clockwork, As a Witness to the Truth Which Consists of Twelve Discussions from One to Twelve O'clock, for Each Hour One Discussion," Noah Good, trans., E. Morris Sider, ed. (unpublished translation from copy of the original document), in Historical Library and Archives, Messiah College.

[13]Stoeffler, *Evangelical Pietism*, pp. 27-29, 96-99; *The New International Dictionary of the Christian Church*, s.v. "Puritans; Puritanism," by Peter Toon; *Mennonite Encyclopedia*, Vol. V, s.v. "Puritanism," by Keith L. Sprunger.

[14]Stoeffler, *Evangelical Pietism*, p. 29.

[15]Carlton O. Wittlinger, *Quest for Piety and Obedience* (Nappanee, Ind.: Evangel Press, 1978), p. 121. Church historian Ted A. Campbell includes under the rubric of the "religion of the heart," in addition to Pietists and Puritans, such other groups as the Quakers, Moravians, Jansenists, Quietists, Scots-Irish Evangelicals, Wesleyan beginnings, Orthodox Piety, and Hasidic Judaism. Ted A. Campbell, *Religion of the Heart*, pp. 2-218. See also Mark A. Noll, *A History of Christianity in the United States* (Grand Rapids, Mich.: William B. Eerdmans, 1992), pp. 83-113, 166-190.

[16]*The Small Davidic Psaltery* was based on a hymnbook with a very similar title published in Europe in 1718 by the radical Pietist group, The Community of True Inspiration. Royce Saltzman indicates that although the influence of this hymnal on the Brethren in Christ cannot be documented, the continuities of the first Brethren in Christ hymnal support the relationship. Royce H. Saltzman, "A Historical Study of the Function of Music Among the Brethren in Christ" (D.M.A. diss., University of Southern California, 1964), pp. 92-99. For *The Small Davidic Psaltery*, see *Brethren Encyclopedia*, s.v. "Kleine Davidische Psatlerspiel der Kinder Zion," by Hedda Raschke Durnbaugh, and *Brethren Encyclopedia*, s.v., "Community of True Inspiration," by Donald F. Durnbaugh.

[17]See *Mennonite Encyclopedia*, Vol. III, s.v. "Martyr's Mirror," by N. van der Zijpp and Harold S. Bender; Brethren Encyclopedia, s.v. "Blutige Schau-Platz oder Maryter Spiegelder Tauffs Gesinnten, Der," by Donald F. Durnbaugh. The latter states: "A frontispiece showing the immersion baptism of Jesus Christ was removed from copies purchased by Mennonites but was favored by German Baptist Brethren buyers. . . ."

[18]*Mennonite Encyclopedia*, Vol. I., s.v. "Ausbund," by Robert Friedmann. See also, Steven M. Nolt, *A History of the Amish* (Intercourse, Pa.: Good Books, 1992), p. 21; Richard K. McMaster, *Land, Piety, Peoplehood*, pp. 143, 169-171. Ausbund means "select" salvation. The *Ausbund* was without notes and the tunes were taken over from secular folk songs.

[19]For the joining of the two traditions, see Alderfer, "The Mind of the Brethren," pp. 79-85; Donald F. Durnbaugh, "Nineteenth-Century Dunker Views of the River Brethren," *Mennonite Quarterly Review* (April 1993), 133-151. Luke L. Keefer, Jr. has written: "Both Anabaptism and Pietism shared the conviction that Protestantism alone did not make one Christian. They both critiqued Protestants who were not genuinely converted. There were affinities between the personal and family piety of the two movements. Both looked to the early church, as depicted in the New Testament, for their model of Christianity, though they emphasized different aspects of the primitive vision. . . . In blending the two traditions, one also changes

them. Anabaptism and Pietism are not like two separate cogwheels in a machine, whose teeth perfectly mesh with each other. Rather, they are more like a mixed fruit drink where both flavors can be identified but achieve a new blended flavor that is not like that of either ingredient. From the beginning, the Brethren in Christ were Anabaptists with a difference. . . . They were Pietists with a difference. . . ." In "The Three Streams in Our Heritage," 29-33.

[20]Robert Friedmann, *Mennonite Piety Through the Centuries* (Goshen, Ind.: Mennonite Historical Society, 1949), pp. 19-34; Theron Schlabach, *Peace, Faith, Nation*, pp. 87-16; MacMaster, *Land, Piety, Peoplehood*, pp. 157-182; *Mennonite Encyclopedia*, Vol. V., s.v. "Pietism," by Cornelius J. Dyck.

[21]*Theological Dictionary, Containing Definitions of All Religious Terms: A Comprehensive View of Every Article in the System of Divinity, and Impartial Account of All the Principal Movements* (Philadelphia: Edwin T. Scott, 1820; first published in England in 1802). See "A Memoir of the Author," *Miscellaneous Works of Rev. Charles Buck*, rev. ed. (New Haven, Conn.: Whitmore and Minor, 18333), pp. 2-65; *Dictionary of National Biography*, Vol. III (1917), s.v. "Buck, Charles," by W.G.B.

[22]The book was printed in Germantown in 1792 by Peter Leibert.

[23]In the eighteenth century, Pietists who separated themselves from the established churches, believed that ecclesiastical organizations inherently militated against true spirituality. For Sauer, such church organizations included sectarian groups such as the German Baptist Brethren. *Brethren Encyclopedia*, s.v. "Separatism," by Dessie M. Myers.

[24]Ibid., s.v. "Sauer (Sower, Saur), Johann Christoph I," by Donald F. Durnbaugh, and ibid., s.v. "Sauer (Sower, Saur), Christopher II," by Donald F. Durnbaugh.

[25]Stephen L. Longenecker, *The Christopher Sauers* (Elgin, Ill.: The Brethren Press, 1981), pp. 51-58; Julius Friedrich Sachse, *The German Sectarian of Pennsylvania*, Vol II (Philadelphia: Published by the author, 1971, AMS reprint of the 1900 edition), pp. 1-68.

[26]*Mennonite Encyclopedia*, Vol. II, s.v. "Froschauer Bible and Testaments," by Adolph Fluri. See also George H. Williams, *The Radical Reformation* (Philadelphia: Westminster Press, 1962), pp. 816-817.

[27]*Mennonite Encyclopedia*, Vol. II, s.v. "Haetzer, Ludwig," by Gerhard Goeters, and s.v. "Denk, Hans," by Christian Neff and Walter Fellmann.

[28]J.C. Wenger, *The Mennonite Church in America* (Scottdale, Pa.: Herald Press, 1966), p. 142; John L. Ruth, *Maintaining the Right Fellowship* (Scottdale, Pa.: Herald Press, 1984), p. 62.

[29]Amos Hoover, letter to the author, December 20, 1990; C.J. Dyck, letter to author, January 22, 1990; J.C. Wenger, letter to author, February 2, 1990.

[30]According to tradition, the Bible was brought to America by Christian Lesher's grandfather or great-grandfather at the time of immigration. See *History of Franklin County, Pennsylvania* (Chicago: Warner, Beers, and Co., 1887), p. 949.

[31]C.W. Boyer, letter to author, September 2, 1986; E.J. Swalm, letter to author, September 10, 1986; also interviews with E. Morris Sider, Arthur Climenhaga, Henry Hostetter, Charlie Byers, Henry Ginder, Luke L. Keefer, Jr.

[32]*Brethren Encyclopedia*, s.v. "Wittgenstein," by Donald F. Durnbaugh, and s.v. "Berleburg," by Donald F. Durnbaugh.

[33]Donald F. Durnbaugh, "Genius of the Brethren," *Brethren Life and Thought* (Winter 1959), 10-18. C. David Ensign, "Radical German Pietism (c.1675-c.1675)" (Ph.D. diss., Boston University, 1955), pp. 290, 291.

[34]The full title of the first volume in English translation reads as follows: *The Holy Scripture, Old and New, Reviewed and Translated According to the Basic Text, Together with Some Helpful Explanations According to the Literal Meaning, As Well as Also the Most Important Types and Figures and Prophecies Relating to Christ and His Kingdom and at the Same Time Some Doctrines about the Conditions of the Churches as They Are Conducted in These Times, Our Last Times, with Which is Blended an Explanation Commentary Which Makes Possible the Purification, Enlightenment, and Unifying with Him God, the Standing of the Inner Life, or the Way and Working of God in the Soul.* Translated by Noah G. Good (modern capitalization used).

[35]*Brethren Encyclopedia*, s.v. "Berleburg Bible," by David R. Hinks; Gerhard Fridrich, "The Brethren and the Berleburg Bible," *Schwarzenau* (April 1940), pp. 5, 6; Martin Brecht, "The Berleburg Bible," *Pietism and Modern Times*, trans. Larry Neff (unpublished, December 1995), pp. 12, 17, 18.

[36]Ensign, "Radical German Pietism," pp. 330-337.

[37]Brecht, "Berleburg Bible," pp. 17-19. O'Malley, *German-American Evangelicalism*, p. 275. *Realencyclopadie für Protestantische Theologie und Kirche*, Vol. 3, s.v. "Berleburg Bibel," trans., Noah G. Good.

[38]Brecht, "Berleburg Bible," pp. 15-18; O'Malley, *German American Evangelicalism*, pp. 271-278; *Realencyclopadie*, "Berleburg Bibel."

[39]Brecht, "Berleburg Bible," pp. 16, 18, 22, 25-27; Ensign, "Radical German Pietism," pp. 326-332; O'Malley, *German-American Pietism*, pp. 276-280, 285-290; C.D. Ensign, letter to author, April 7, 1999; William G. Willoughby, letters to author, May 25, June 4, November 19, 1999.

[40]F. Ernest Stoeffler, ed., *Continental Pietism and Early American Christianity* (Grand Rapids, Mich.: William B. Eerdmans, 1976), p. 272; James Tanis, *Dutch Pietism in the Middle Colonies* (The Hague, Netherlands: Martinus Nijhoff, 1967), pp. 1-197.

[41]Interview with Peter C. Erb, October 16, 1995; E.G. Alderfer, *The Ephrata Commune, An Early American Counterculture* (Pittsburgh: University of Pittsburgh Press, 1985), p. 91; O'Malley, *German-American Evangelicalism*, pp. 271-290; J. Steven O'Malley, letter to author, December 5, 1995.

[42]Ensign, "Radical German Pietism," p. 290; D. Durnbaugh, "Genius of the Brethren," pp. 10-18; John S. Flory, *Literary Activity of the German Baptist Brethren* (Elgin, Ill.: Brethren Publications House, 1908); Donald F. Durnbaugh, letter to the author, September 15, 1986; Ruth Greenwalt, letter to the author, April 21, 1992.

[43]For this development, see Wittlinger, *Quest for Piety and Obedience*, pp. 18-21; Martin H. Schrag, "The Brethren in Christ Attitude Towards the World" (Ph.D. diss., Temple University, 1967), pp. 11-21.

[44]*Brethren Encyclopedia*, s.v. "Antietam (Price) Church of the Brethren," by Mary Landis Rice; Martin H. Schrag, "The Life and Times of Christian Lesher," *Brethren in Christ History and Life* (April 1995), 75-78; J. Lindwood Eisenbert, ed., *A History of the Church of the Brethren in the Southern District of Pennsylvania* (Quincy, Pa.: Quincy Orphanage, 1941, reprinted in 1966), pp. 7, 8; Charles W. Treher, "Snow Hill Cloister," *Publications of the Pennsylvania-German Society*, Vol. II (Allentown, Pa.: The Pennsylvania-German Society, 1968), pp. 26-30, 74-103; *Brethren Encyclopedia*, s.v. "Snow Hill Community," by Jobie E. Riley.

The Church and Church Discipline

Christian Lesher's essay on the church and church discipline, written in 1841, was the first of three major works from the bishop's pen. Its long title (typical of nineteenth-century titles) in English reads: *Witness to the Truth: A Clear Understanding According to God's Word on How God's Children in the Fellowship of Christ Are to Keep House and Order Among Themselves.* The entire work was published after Lesher's death in three issues of the *Evangelical Visitor* in 1904.[1] The context of the writing is not known, but the essay implies that Lesher composed it at the time when he was involved in discipline issues. The essay relates closely to the statement on discipline that he sent to the Canadian members in 1844.[2] This essay, however, is his most developed work on the subject.

In keeping with his theological posture, Lesher notes that in "keeping order," love will prevail. True conversions, he maintains, will result in a harmonious community. Conversion will lead to following Christ's example in baptism, which, in turn, makes one part of the visible church. Baptism symbolizes the forgiveness of sins which are buried in the blood of Christ; the person is now resurrected to newness of life and daily mortifies the deeds of the flesh.[3]

Those who have spiritually "supped" with Christ through the Spirit will want to commune with fellow believers, according to the command established by Jesus Christ and the apostles. Christ's command to wash feet (John 13) is a manifestation of Christian oneness, and of love for and submission to others. Caring for one another in "sincere and fervent love" is taught in Matthew 18: 15-18, which verses also involve disciplining when necessary, such action being sometimes necessary because humans are subject to "many infirmities."

Lesher instructs the reader, if tempted to look at objects that excite evil desire, to turn to the "inward presence of God," praying for power to resist the evil. If "inordinate inclinations" move one to go to ungodly places, or to covetously seek to gain "great profits by buying, selling or trading," one should turn to God, realizing that the "vanity and riches" of this world can shift one's love from God. If one's evil disposition causes one "to touch or do anything inordinately," again turn to God to receive the true power against the dangers. And if one is enticed to speak with a tongue "full of deadly poison," remember that one will be judged for every unrepented word idly spoken. God can tame the tongue: if people are truly alert, praying, and watching before God, they can gain help to overcome temptation.

In this self examination, Lesher is concerned with both inner attitudes and outer actions. Such inter-relatedness was important to groups like the German Baptist Brethren and the Mennonites. Lesher's reference to the "inward presence of God" is in keeping with Pietism; his concern with the dangers of great profits from business transactions illustrate Anabaptist/Mennonite views on separation from the world. In keeping with both traditions, Lesher believed that spiritual and ethical victory is possible but not easily realized.

But, Lesher continues, some Christians do not "pluck out their evil eye" or "cut off their feet" (metaphorically speaking) with the result that they become carnal and spiritually dead. It then becomes the task of the church to cut them off. Such disciplining, however, must be done caringly because there are two levels of sin—venial (minor) sins and mortal (major) sins, which must be dealt with in different fashions.

Venial sins, inconsiderate acts rooted in a lack of spiritual alertness, are to be handled according to the three steps described in Matthew 18: 15-18. If some member trespasses in "small matters" and no one else knows about it, tell no one but approach the trespasser in "lowliness and meekness," after having carefully prayed about the matter. The reproving must be gentle in nature, modeled on Jesus' teaching that one must be ready to forgive a fellow believer seven times a day. Lesher also quotes early church fathers (whom he does not identify) who taught that if one reproves without having previously prayed, one is an "unmerciful father."

If the sinner does not listen to the reproof, he or she is not yet to be exposed. Instead, one or two "well spoken [of]" Brethren should accompany the first person so that the truth can be established. If there is no repentance, the church is to hear the case. If there is a change of heart, the offender is to be forgiven; if not, he is to be considered a heathen and a publican.

Such action, however, is not full excommunication, because Jesus himself ate and drank with publicans and sinners. But at the same time, the offender is not to greet others with the holy kiss, take communion, or wash the feet of other members. If he repents, experiences grace and forgiveness, he is to be brought back into the fold, but only "by the council of the Church." Thus all members of the local congregation or local district have a voice in determining the return of the disciplined person, not just the clergy.

Lesher next discusses how to deal with someone who has committed a venial sin against a non-member, which sin becomes general knowledge, or who does some "inordinate act"that becomes public knowledge. In such cases, it is not necessary to follow Matthew 18, but brotherly love requires personal interaction with the offender by one or two brethren. The offender who repents must make a public confession (apparently in a Sunday morning worship service) to "remove from the world the stumbling block and offense which he gave." But if that person does not repent, he is to be treated as a publican and sinner (by what has been called the lesser ban). From Lesher's commentary, it is clear that members wanted the outside world to know that they were a community of integrity.

Lesher adds that if persons guilty of venial sin (or moral sin) remain "refactory and finally embrace objections against the Church or even go so far as to calumniate the word of God," they should be excommunicated. A letter is to be sent throughout the church informing members that they are not to have fellowship with the excommunicated.

Lesher next takes up what he calls the "most dangerous sin of all": "disagreement and disunion" within the church. Such a sin is Satin's "greatest masterpiece," a "hellish weed." Those who have experienced disunity know its demonic nature. Lesher notes that Jesus, his apostles, and the "ancient fathers" warned about this great danger, and he supports his strong statements by Scripture (Eph. 4:3;

John 17:21, 13:35; Rom. 12:9, 10, 16; 1 Cor. 1:10; Phil. 2:2, 3, 5; James 4:7; 2 Cor. 13:11).[4] Thus he brings the weight of the New Testament against those who are divisive.

In keeping with his regard for the authority of the early church fathers, Lesher quotes Clement of Rome and Ignatius for support. The writings of both men were in the Berleburg Bible, although Lesher may have found the passages quoted in some other source, such as the writings of Gottfried Arnold. Clement, prominent Roman presbyter-bishop, in writing to the Corinthian Christians castigates them for their quarreling and dissensions, activities diametrically contrary to the spirit, thought, and end of Christianity as shown in Matthew 26:24.[5]

Lesher quotes from two letters of Ignatius, Bishop of Antioch who wrote seven letters to various churches on the way to Rome where he was executed for being a Christian. In his letter to the Philadelphians, Ignatius calls on his readers to guard against those who cause dissentions. Those belonging to Jesus Christ will be of the same mind with the overseer (or bishop). Seditious persons will not inherit the Kingdom of God.

In Lesher's second quotation from Ignatius, the early church father states that nothing of importance, such as baptism or the love feast, should be done apart from the bishop. Ignatius identifies the church with the bishop/overseer when he says that "where the overseer appears there is also the church."[6] Lesher does not explain his own understanding of the relationship between the church and the bishop. Does he see the bishops as a group (or only the senior bishop) the custodians of correct belief and practice? As normally understood, such custodianship is contrary to believers church polity: the final authority is in the congregation or total body of believers.

Those who have experienced the damage that can be done by strife and division can understand why Lesher cited so many sources. Lesher urges, with Apostle Paul, that Christians are to keep a sharp watch because "grievous" wolves will cause disunion and draw disciples away with seemingly good words but unsound doctrine, not out of love for the Lord but for the sake of their "belly." Lesher asks the church to discern that what is being said and taught is of God, not of men. The situation is all the more dangerous, he maintains, when unfaithful people "are humble in their outward conduct and are irreproachable in their walk and conversation . . . and have the appearance of virtue." (Is Lesher referring to some Brethren in Christ who were more conservative than he was?) Such people claim they are upholding "evangelical doctrine" and calling on people to obey the gospel.

The only thing to do with such people, Lesher declares, is to withdraw from them; otherwise we may share in their sin. These people "build Babylon." It is as Luther translated Titus 3:10, 11, "A man that is a heretic reject."

Having concluded to reject the sowers of dissension, Lesher attempts to determine which of them are guilty of venial sins, which of mortal sins. In Lesher's opinion, the "leaders of division" are more guilty than their followers. Whatever the nature of their sin, these leaders, if they come to our meetings, are not to speak publicly, nor are we to attend their meetings. We can have non-religious interaction with them—shake hands, eat and drink with them, as we do with all "heathen and publicans." As long as no mortal sin is committed, we should never see them as enemies; rather our approach to them should be in a spirit of meekness, admonishing and reproving them with the hope of restoring them to full fellowship.

Lesher illustrates his point with an analogy to a person who is physically sick. We do all we can to nurse that person back to health. If the person dies, however, we bury him, not only because of the bad odor that follows death but also because the body may infect healthy people. Likewise, those who commit mortal sins are to be fully excluded from the family of God. (Some of the mortal sins are listed by Paul in 1 Cor. 5:11 and by John in 2 John. 9, 10, 11.)

When a member has committed mortal sin, Lesher continues, there is no need to follow Matthew 18: the procedure is to make a "most distant separation" from the member. The faithful are not to eat at the same table with those who are fully banned (a separate table can be set for them), or shake hands with them because this is a form of salutation. The fully excommunicated are not to be received in the home as brethren, but it is permissible to "entertain them as strangers." If they are in physical need (lacking clothing or food), they are to be aided lest one be guilty of not loving enemies. In banning persons, we are true to Scripture; we warn members of the dangers of sin, we bring sinners to their senses, thus to repentance.

To accent the need to publicly rebuke those guilty of mortal sins, Lesher quotes Timothy 5: 20, 21 and follows with the Berleburg Bible commentary on these two verses. Here the emphasis is placed on public rebuking as a means of securing repentance, of fulfilling God's desire for a pure church, and of assuring the making of objective judgements instead of allowing emotions or relationships with relatives to influence decisions. He concludes this section by noting that one partakes of the sin if it is passed over in silence, and by instructing that a fair hearing be given, including the two parties to the issue meeting face to face.[7]

Lesher admits that the distinction between venial and mortal sins may sometimes be difficult to define because both the intention and the outer act must be considered. Venial sins, or sins of infirmity (passions of anger, carnal love, fleshly lusts, stealing, etc.) to which all humans are subject, are also common among Christians. Young men in Christ, having overcome Satan, should move beyond such sins; fathers in Christ, having fully mortified the flesh and now living godly lives, are in a position to be a "type and example," showing to all believers "how they should follow after holiness and speed unto perfection."

But alas, Lesher exclaims, even fathers of the faith can commit both venial and mortal sins. This inclination to sin can become a passion, which can be inflamed by the devil's "fiery darts." At first, the human will agree with the conscience that the act is not to be done, but soon the will weakens, paying less attention to the conscience. The "excitement of the flesh" will increase, the senses will be darkened, and finally the will is imprisoned. In that state, sin cannot be resisted.

This leads Lesher to a more precise definition of the two types of sin. If true repentance is effected and there is a firm resolve to be more watchful, the sin committed is venial (one of infirmity), even if it appears to be mortal. On the other hand, what may appear to be a small sin is in fact mortal if it is "repeatedly, willfully, and intentionally committed with a hardened mind," to the extent that there is no uneasiness, all the more so if they are very evil sins, such as mentioned in 1 Corinthians 5:9, 10 and Galatians 5:19-21.

Lesher ends his essay by repeating in summary form the process of Matthew 18 and emphasizing that enforcing either limited or full excommunication can be done only by the church as a body, not by the clergy alone.

NOTES

[1]The dates for the three *Evangelical Visitor* articles are June 1, June 15, and July 15. The articles, originally in German, were translated into English for the paper's readers. The translator is unknown.

[2]See the first chapter for the 1844 statement.

[3]*Evangelical Visitor*, June 1, 1904, p. 14.

[4]Lesher's use of the expression "The Lord Jesus and the Apostles" as a designation for the New Testament implies relating to persons—the persons behind the written Word. "Lord" as a title for Jesus accents his authority, thus one to be followed and obeyed.

[5]*Evangelical Visitor*, June 15, 1904, p. 15. Lesher identifies the author with the Clement mentioned in Philippians 4:3, a view not accepted by contemporary scholars. Clement's letter to the Corinthians was considered Scripture by some of the early church fathers and was included in some early New Testaments: see *International Dictionary of the Christian Church* (1974), s.v. "Clement of Rome," by D.F. Wright.

[6]Citing Acts 11:26, Lesher suggests that Ignatius was converted around A.D. 40 when Paul and Barnabas came to Antioch. He also states that some historians believed that Ignatius was the child that Jesus set in the midst of his disciples (Mark 9:36). Present-day scholars reject such an interpretation.

[7]*Evangelical Visitor*, July 1, 1904, p. 4. Although Lesher uses quotation marks on material taken from the Berleburg Bible, he actually weaves together individual statements into a flowing text. He also amplifies the text at a few places.

A Small Spiritual Magazine [or Storehouse]

A second work by Christian Lesher, entitled in English translation, is *A Small Spiritual Magazine As a Witness to the Truth*.[1] He wrote the book in 1847 at seventy-two years of age and published it in 1849. An oral tradition holds that the Brethren in Christ initially opposed the book's publication, but later reluctantly allowed Lesher to proceed with its printing.[2]

The book deals with theological issues: the incarnation, man's fall and Christ's work of redemption, children and salvation, predestination and free will, and eschatology. Still, Lesher's experiential concerns are very apparent in the volume.

Preface

Lesher explains in the Preface that he undertook the writing of the book because forty-six years earlier (around 1803) he was "transported" by God's grace "from darkness to light . . . from the power of Satan . . . into the redemption of Christ." Once blind, "now I see" (John 9:25). Having had a crisis conversion experience, Lesher says that he sought to walk in the light, which sometimes he did less fully than at other times. But as God gave him more insight and comprehension, he began to put his thoughts on paper.

He came to see that there was great confusion within so-called Christianity, even though many claimed their views were based on Scripture. Their error was deceptive reasoning: Protestant Orthodoxy centered on mental assent to rationalistically stated doctrines, in contrast to experiential faith. His book is to lead others away from the former to the latter.[3] (Lesher's crisis conversion experience, his flexibility regarding individual experience, and his emphasis on personal spiritual growth clearly show the impact of Pietism on him and his writing.)

At the end of his Preface, Lesher prays for his readers that "God may show us the way (Ps. 86:11) and lead us into the truth (John 16:13) making us strong so that we may deny ourselves worldly lusts and all that is unnecessary, to live morally, righteously, and in a godly way in truth until the end."[4] Between his preface and the first chapter, he quotes some Scripture, and includes a poem or hymn which appears to be of his own composition. In English translation, it reads:

Always honor the Scriptures
They are your fortune on earth,
And there, in eternity,
They will be your fortune in heaven.

The one who gets born again here,
As the Scriptures tell us,
and who carries in self denial
The cross of Christ:

And dies daily to himself
Through the power of Christ
Will receive an inheritance
In heaven with him.

Therefore, pay no attention
To the mocking of the one who hates the Bible.
The word he now belittles
Remains the Word of God.

Chapter One
The Incarnation of Christ

Lesher begins the chapter by saying that being in a dark frame of mind a few weeks before Christmas, he prayed to God for a Christmas blessing. On Christmas day, however, he awoke in pain and alternating between being hot and cold, as if he had a fever. His reaction was to think, "O God, is this the Christmas blessing you want to give me?" But on a short reflection, he realized that God was chastising him because he had such a depraved and resistant nature. Then he rejoiced and thanked God for his grace, which was followed by an "unspeakable love" for God and Christ. He rejoiced that Jesus suffered and died for such a poor sinner as Christian Lesher.

In this Christmas experience, he relates, God gave him a deeper understanding of the conception, birth, and nature of Jesus. The experience was so meaningful that the next day he had recovered from his illness. He decided to put on paper the event and the insights he gained from it in order not to forget the richness of it.

Lesher's starting point is that the conception and birth of Jesus was the greatest event that ever occurred because it united deity and humanity in one person. But there has been too much rationalistic speculation regarding the relationship of the two natures. The result has been that some have denied Jesus' deity while others in response have denied his humanity. Such distortions and dissensions hinder God's redemptive work. Lesher's concern is how the two natures were necessary for Christ to make full provision for salvation, holy discipleship, and the harmonious community.

According to Lesher, the deity of Christ has been denied or distorted in various ways. Some believed that Jesus Christ was not God, only the son of God, thus making him less than God. Others reasoned that only after he was baptized did Jesus partake of divinity. A few have said that Jesus was only a prophet. But those who deny the divinity of Christ do not have a firm foundation for the work of redemption, because no human, not even the greatest (Enoch, Moses, Elijah) can save another human, let alone making provision for the entire human race.

Some have denied the deity of Christ, Lesher continues, on the basis of such Scriptures as "My father is greater than I" (John 14:28), and the Father is "greater than all" (John 10:29). But such thinking is foolish and a gangerous perversion, showing only that the person thinking in this fashion does not really know Christ. When Jesus uttered the words, "The father is greater than I," he was not attempting to explain the union he had with the father, but to indicate that in his stay on earth he had some limitations.[5]

Lesher concedes that there was some functional subordination of Jesus to God, as when the angels ministered to Jesus following the temptation, when he was in agony in Gethsemane, and in his obedience unto death. At his death, the Godhead withdrew from Jesus so that he died fully as a man for men, because God cannot die, thus the words, "My God, My God, why have you forsaken me" (Matt. 27:46). Neither during his ministry was Jesus all-knowing (e.g., he did not know when the world would end). Thus Jesus had some limitations during the incarnation.

At the same time, we realize that in certain situations when it was necessary for Jesus to know something to fulfill his mission, the father, through the inner oneness with Jesus Christ, revealed understandings that were beyond human knowledge, as when Jesus knew the most secret thoughts of people (Matt. 9:4 and John 2:25). Such knowledge and other testimonies clearly show the interior union that Jesus had with the Father through his deity. It is as John wrote: Jesus Christ, the Son, "is the true God" (1 John 5:20). Thus in a summary manner, Lesher lays down the general principle grounded in nature: a son is of the same essence as his father. Every essence manifests its essence.

But there are those, Lesher continues, who so much emphasize Christ's deity that they deny his humanity. Some do so when they claim that Christ did not receive his humanity from Mary; rather he brought pure humanity from heaven (celestial flesh), and, although nurtured by Mary, in effect he passed through Mary, somewhat like water passing through a pipe.

Although he mentions no names, Lesher is known to have read Menno Simons, and very likely knew that this early Anabaptist believed in the celestial flesh doctrine. He may also have read other Dutch Anabaptists such as Dirk Philips, and early German Baptist Brethren leaders Michael Frantz and Alexander Mack, Sr., all of whom agreed with Menno Simons.[6] The supposed point of the doctrine was to insure the sinlessness of Jesus, but the result was to deny the full humanity of Jesus. Such docetic belief (Jesus only appeared to be but was not really human) was condemned by the early church. Lesher rejected it also.[7]

Closely related to the docetic belief was the one described by Lesher which held that because Jesus Christ was fully divine, he could not have suffered and died—it only appeared that he did so. In the first Christian centuries, a few people believed that matter (flesh and blood) was inherently evil. To such people, suffering was highly deplorable and meant defeat. But, Lesher argues, Christ's suffering and death was essential to provide for forgiveness of sins and to set an example of self denial. Satan tries to convince people that Christ's suffering was not necessary, thus they think that they do not need to deny themselves in obedient discipleship. But the truth is that those who believe that Christ did not suffer and die have no sacrifice for their sins. Christ becoming man was foundational to the new birth.

The humanity of Jesus was clearly manifested in his life. He experienced all the senses and emotions of humans. He knew and identified with people's infirmities and sorrows. Certainly Jesus saw himself as human. He repeatedly identified himself as the "Son of Man."

Lesher accents Christ's humanity by his interpretation of some Old Testament prophecies and their fulfillment in Jesus. Already in the garden there is reference to the "seed" (descendant of woman), which is carried through the Old Testament, as in Abraham, David, and Isaiah. Jesus saw himself as the "offspring of David" (Rev. 22:16), and Paul recognized that Jesus was "born after the seed of David" (Rom. 1:3, 4; 9:5). The family line not only indicated human lineage and implied the humanity of Jesus, but also pointed to one human who is to be the fulfillment of God's salvation work.

Lesher also believes that Christ's humanity was shown in his willingness to call Christians his brothers. Those who accept Christ through the Spirit and allow themselves to be led into sanctification become his brothers after the Spirt and will live with him eternally. By being a fellow brother, Jesus emphasized the human commonality between Christ and Christians.

To explain the miracle of God and man being united in one person, Lesher refers to the account of the angel Gabriel informing Mary of the coming conception. Being a "chaste, pure, hallowed and . . . undefiled Virgin," Mary could not understand how this could happen. Gabriel informed her that her conception would not happen through the "sinful seed of man" but through the everlasting imperishable seed, "the living Word of God" (1 Pet. 1:23). The Holy Ghost would come on her and prepare her for the miraculous conception. Mary believed and gave her heart, her whole being, with its disposition, lusts and appetites, over to God's will. Then the Holy Spirit came on Mary "completely hallowing her," and at the same time blocked and sealed the fountain of the Adamic sinful nature, with its thoughts, preferences, lusts and appetites. As a result, Mary's motivations and actions were determined by pure, holy human nature, all evil tendencies having been purified by God. Thus the sinlessness of Jesus was maintained by the Holy Spirit sanctifying the maiden.

Lesher highlights the nature of the Word entering Mary. The Word was with the Father before the foundation of the world; the Word is the power of the Most High; the Word is God through whom all things were made. This Word entered Mary and received from Mary pure and holy humanity. Thus the godly nature was brought into the human; both natures were substantially united in Christ.

Lesher attempted to present a trustworthy understanding of the incarnation—how the human and divine natures were related and integrated in Jesus Christ. Both natures are essential to God's work of salvation. One nature must not be emphasized at the expense of the other nature. The incarnation was not to reveal a fully logical theology; rather, it was to bring about the salvation of sinners and to issue in a commitment to follow Christ.

Chapter 2
The Fall and the Restoration of Humanity in Jesus Christ

In this chapter, Lesher considers the nature of humans, the need for the new birth, the nature of holy discipleship, and the church's role in fostering corporate piety. He uses the parable of the Good Samaritan as his scriptural base, quoting the passage (Luke 10; 24-38) in full. He points out that the lawyer with whom Jesus spoke knew what the law required—to fully love God and his neighbor (as did the priest and the Levite). But the Jews, given to pharisaical self-righteousness, thought that they alone were God's chosen people, thus only fellow Jews were their neighbors. The result was that, following their fleshly nature, the Samaritans responded in kind.[8]

Jesus wanted to teach the lawyer that even a Samaritan can love God and responsibly love his neighbor. Sectarian love is not enough for God: one is to love even one's enemies.[9]

In a spiritual sense, Lesher suggests, Jerusalem is the holy city, Jericho a cursed city (Josh. 6:26). In a spiritual sense, when one moves toward the cursed city, one will fall among evil spirits who will entice one towards "the lust of the flesh, the lust of the eyes, and the pride of life" (1 John 2:16). Although once wearing the clothes of righteousness, now one is in a half-dead condition; one still has some love for God, but not enough to secure a firm foundation. In such a state, neither cold nor hot, the backslider needs the loving Samaritan (Jesus Christ) to pour wine (cleansing) and oil (comfort of the Holy Spirit) and be returned to God's congregation (*gemeinschaft*).[10]

Lesher next considers the parable from what he identifies as the scriptural way of holiness. Some ancient church father, he notes, believed that the man attacked and left as half dead represents the fall of Adam. But Lesher claims that this is a serious misreading because Adam and his posterity were *fully* dead. Unfortunately, some so-called Christians today think that only what is needed to be Christian is to leave gross sins and bad habits behind, become respectable and practice the outer forms of Christianity (be baptized, take communion, attend church services), and accept the pastor's word that their sins are forgiven.

But this makes the way of holiness far too superficial. Such people make the same mistake as the characters in the parable, namely, thinking that they are justified by the deeds of the law, by going through the outer practices of the faith. What they need is the new birth and a "faith which worketh by love" (Gal. 5:6).[11]

Lesher's concern is not to set aside the law but to emphasize that salvation is by grace, not works, and that only the truly converted have the inner heart condition to lovingly do God's will and follow his commandments.

Lesher now moves to describe the nature of the soul. That Adam and Eve died spiritually when they ate the forbidden fruit but continued to live physically for several hundred years implies that man has a soul that never dies. In contrast, animals have a soul that dies, as shown by their body and soul dying at the same time (support for which Lesher finds in the Berleburg and Froschauer translations).[12]

Evidence of humans being unique (with an undying soul) is the trichotomous nature of God's creation. Lesher makes much of the creation account in Genesis where three different works are used to describe God's work: "and God *created*," "and God *said*," "and God *made*." This not only shows a tripartite creation but also, and more importantly, that all three key words were used in the creation of humans. All three words clearly show that man has a higher source of creation and is the most noble of all the creatures. Man is made in the three-fold image of God (body, soul, and spirit). Whether Jacob Boehme's belief that a trinity of principles underlies all of reality influenced Lesher in these views is not known but the possibility is plausible.[13]

Lesher also believed that the souls of animals were created, the source of creation being the world-energy spirit or ether (*dustgeist*). When an animal dies, both its body and soul cease to exist, in contrast to humans. Man is an "undying living entity," his soul not created or fashioned by God but coming out of eternity and "breathed into by God," thus made in God's image.[14]

The spirit in humans is identified by Lesher in several terms, the most common of which are conscience, spirit, and mind. He usually sees the soul indwelling the body, and the spirit indwelling the soul. How the three interacted determined whether one was saved or unsaved.

Lesher notes a sequence in the sins that led to the fall: first, the body lusted to eat the fruit, then the soul consented, finally the spirit did not resist. When Eve ate and did not immediately die, she gave some fruit to Adam, who ate it. Adam and Eve's original godly nature disappeared, because that nature cannot live in a wicked soul or sinful body. The couple experienced the inner turmoil that comes from sinning. They now knew that they were without power to resist temptation. No longer having free fruit to eat, they not only had to plow and plant but also to struggle against weeds and thistles. Many poisonous things began to grow. Animals, at one time companionable, became wild and killed each other. The entire world became perverted; humankind became sinful, ever tempted by lust and pride (1 John 2:16). Existence, he concludes, is as the

Froschauer Bible translates James 3:15: "earthly, beastly, and devilish."

Yet, already in the garden, hope was given in the promise of one who would overcome evil. A sign of the hope was God's clothing Adam and Eve with skins, a foreshadowing of people with a coat of righteousness (Jesus Christ), the garment of holiness, which was lost in Paradise. Jesus came to make provision for humans to regain the divine nature lost in the fall.

Human response to God's offer of salvation begins with the awakening of the dead conscience. The conscience, with a very limited hearing potential, is awakened by the "salutary grace of God," somewhat like a person half asleep who hears the sounds of words but does not fully understand them. Most people suppress or stifle the call but others allow themselves to hear the words, "Awake thou that sleepeth, and arise from the dead, and Christ shall give you light" (Eph. 5:14). They realize they are sinners, and, being under the convicting power of the Holy Spirit, feel a true fear of God. The angels lead them to true heartfelt repentance as they humble themselves and, cooperating with God, "work out their salvation with fear and trembling" (Phil. 2:12). They accept the invitation to fully surrender themselves to God's grace.[15]

In conversion or regeneration, the godly nature retakes its place in the conscience or spirit of humans. The result is an emotional experience: inner communion, joy, and assurance as the Holy Spirit witnesses to our Spirit. In regeneration, the godly nature "will again enliven and rule the spirit of man by its complete supremacy. The spirit of man will enliven and rule the soul, the soul will enliven, govern and rule the body so that the spirit, soul and body may be sanctified through and through" (1 Thess. 5:23).[16]

Lesher now returns more directly to the Good Samaritan parable, further interpreting it in a spiritual sense, and developing the idea of Christ as the Good Samaritan. It was Christ's compassion in seeing our wretchedness that brought him into the world. He continues to knock on the door of our hearts. When he finds someone who feels the wounds of sins and asks for grace and forgiveness, Christ pours the oil and wine into the wounds. The oil represents the comfort of the Holy Spirit, the forgiveness of sins, the Christ-created living faith, and the joy of salvation. Although all desire the oil, few want the "sharp, purifying, sanctifying wine," but without "holiness no one will see God" (Heb. 12:14). Finally, Christ dresses the wounds with the "bandage of love."[17]

In the parable, the Samaritan placed the wounded man on his donkey and brought him to an inn. Physically, Lesher says, the donkey is only an animal, but spiritually he is like Jesus who carried the sins of the world. Lesher quotes Isaiah 53:4-6 (becoming "wounded for our transgressions") and 1 Peter 2:24 (Jesus carrying "our sins in his own body on the tree") to substantiate his statement.

Lesher sees the inn to which the Samaritan took the wounded man in two spiritual ways. First, it illustrates that those on the "new and living way" have innermost fellowship with the Father and the Son, and spiritual fellowship with all others whose sins have been cleansed—the church. Second, the inn points believers to God leading the born again into the outer visible church of Jesus Christ, there to be nurtured and edified by one another.

The intention of Jesus to build the visible fellowship, Lesher holds, is shown in the manner in which the Lord led Paul to conversion. Jesus could have done it for Paul, but God wanted Paul to get acquainted with Ananias and other believers who would lead him to baptism and bring him into the visible church. The Lord did the same thing to Cornelius and his household: as soon as the group was baptized by the Holy Spirit, they were baptized by water and brought into the church. The same thing happened to the Ethiopian eunuch and to many others.

These examples show that it is God's plan to bring all his people into one community and one faith so that all believers are one, even as God the Father and God the Son are one. In the body of Christ there is neither Jew nor Greek, neither slave nor freeman, neither male nor female for all are one; all have been baptized "through one Spirit," and "all made to drink of one Spirit." Unfortunately, most Christians have not done well in being one, with the result that the church is not like the church described in Acts 4:32.[18]

The goal of a visible church is also basic to understanding the role of the inn's host and the two coins the Samaritan gave to the host to care for the wounded man. The host, as interpreted by Lesher, is the teacher/minister, and the two coins are the Bible and the "inward Spirit of God."

Lesher offers instructions on the responsibilities of the minister, basing his comments on several biblical passages.[19] He is to care for those whom Christ has brought to him; in doing this he is to "preach the word . . . rebuke . . . admonish . . . endure afflictions . . . edify . . . do the work of an evangelical preacher . . . and conduct . . . his office unrightly." The minister is to work without favoritism. The purpose of his ministry is to prepare the saints to perform their service so that Christ's community can be built up toward oneness in faith and doctrine. The end is fully developed persons who measure up to the perfection of Christ, who, when properly matured, will be firm in the truth, will reject deceptive doctrine and selfish desires, assume responsibilities, abstain from iniquity, and give themselves to holiness.[20]

Innkeepers have helpers and so do leaders of the church who have duties to fulfill. Such helpers are not to engage in scolding; they are to be friendly to everyone, teachable, and able to deal gently with sinners. Those who are arrogant are to be rebuked for the sake of their souls.

"Everyone," Lesher concludes, "in the house of God is to be helpful as he is able, and to do his part in taking care of the weak and sick. Out of heartfelt love one for another, we are to care for one another and watch out for one another. Where we see that anyone is walking into danger of injury or of contracting disease, we are to warn and counsel against it and help one another to find the way again. . . ."[21]

Lesher ends the chapter by quoting six Bible passages that deal with redemptive church discipline. Those who want a further explanation he refers to his 1841 essay on the subject.

In summary, the major concerns in this second chapter are the centrality of the new birth, the depth of human depravity, the trichotomous nature of humans, the godly nature that was lost in the fall but restored in the new birth, the restored godly nature as the basis for holy living and integral to the harmonious church.

Elements of both Anabaptism and Pietism can be seen in this chapter. Both believed in the necessity of a new birth, the new nature enabling Christ-like living. Both believed in the importance of the small group to enrich and discern the way. The Pietists emphasized feeling, the Anabaptists in following in the footsteps of

Jesus. Lesher believed that persons outside of Christ are spiritually dead, whereas the Anabaptists believed that something of the image of God remained in fallen humans.[22]

Speculation regarding the constitution of humans was especially related to radical Pietism. Jacob Boehme believed that all creation was tripartite in nature, including the creator God. The Berleburg Bible dealt with dichotomy and trichotomy regarding human nature. Lesher's understanding of humans was very similar to that of Gottfriend Arnold. Lesher related his belief in the pre-existence of the soul to his trichotomous view of humans.[23]

Chapter Three
The Salvation of Innocent Children

In this chapter, Christian Lesher considers the issue of children who die before the age of accountability. The controversy over infant baptism, so strong in Reformation Europe, carried over to North America. That Lesher's area of Chambersburg was no stranger to the controversy is shown by articles on the subject published by the German Reformed church papers *The Weekly Messenger* and *Kirchen-Zeitung*, both printed in Chambersburg. These articles supported infant baptism and rejected adult baptism and the immersion mode.[24]

Deeply concerned by the many interpretations regarding baptism, Lesher went to the Bible to find the truth. To explain his understanding of baptism he posed the following four basic statements, then dealt with each statement separately:

1. Some believe that all who die before they are baptized will be lost;

2. Some believe that because of original sin, those who die before they are baptized must go through a long and painful process of purification and purgatory, and suffer much before they are saved;

3. Some believe that only the children of believing parents will be saved, that children of unbelieving parents will be lost;

4. Some believe that all innocent children will be saved through the merits, blood, and sacrifice of Jesus Christ.[25]

In addressing the first statement, Lesher uses the *Martyr's Mirror* as authority to establish that infant baptism as a means of securing salvation was the practice as early as the third century.[26] He quotes the Anabaptist Menno Simons (1496-1561) to show that in Reformation times almost everyone believed in infant baptism. But Menno Simons believed that such baptism was a "work of hypocrisy" (a common sixteenth-century Anabaptist designation for infant baptism), because true baptism means a basic change of the inner person from the evil to the good, from a fleshly to a spiritual nature.[27]

Lesher develops this point by noting that whether a new birth is physical or spiritual, a new life emerges. Whether baptized or not, children do not have a godly nature. Baptism does not bring new birth, for proof of which Lesher refers to Simon the Sorcerer (Acts 8:9-23), who although baptized was sharply rebuked by Peter because his heart was not right with God.[28]

He next examines "on the scale of holiness" the belief that infant baptism replaced the Old Testament practice of circumcision. But this view, he asserts, is not correct because Abraham was declared righteous before he was circumcised; circumcision was a sign and seal of his righteousness by faith, and an indication that he was to be the father of all who believe by faith (Rom. 4:3,10,11).

In the same manner, baptism is the sign and seal of the righteousness by faith received before baptism, as stated in Mark 16:16. This relates well to the baptism of Simon, who, although baptized, had yet to hear the reason for his rebuke. Thus Apostle Peter wrote that the washing off of physical dirt does not save; rather salvation is rooted in a pledge made to God from a clear conscience through the resurrection of Jesus Christ.

Lesher summarizes these thoughts by affirming that when we have new life in Christ and have made the commitment to God, based on a good conscience, we have the faith of Abraham which saves us and qualifies us to be baptized. But since minor children do not have the new life in Christ, have not made a commitment, and do not know evil from righteousness, they are not qualified to be baptized. Understandably, neither Jesus nor his disciples commanded the baptism of children.[29]

He next considers the view that infants must be baptized to remove, or deal with, original sin. He agrees that children inherit original sin; it has been passed on from Adam and Eve by physical birth to all their descendants. He also agrees that something must be done to overcome its consequences and to free us from its hold.

But to believe that baptism removes original sin is wrong and manifests the perversion caused by original sin. It is also wrong to think that one can wash away original sin by human hands with a little water. It is easy to see that the lust of the eye, the lust of the flesh, and the proud spirit, as well as many inner sins, all coming from original sin, are as evident in baptized infants as in unbaptized ones.

It is a great disrespect to Christ's blood to believe that baptism takes away from original sin, Lesher insists. And it is significant that there is not one word in the New Testament or in the first two centuries regarding the practice of infant baptism: the Christians of those centuries had a right understanding of the meaning of the cross.[30]

Using *Martyr's Mirror*, Lesher focuses on the views of early church father Tertullian (around 160-220) who was concerned that some Christians baptized their children at a young age. But why hurry innocent children, he asked, for Jesus invited such children to come to him. Children must gain understanding, be taught and instructed in the faith, to know Christ before they come for baptism. People should prepare for baptism by fasting, praying, confessing their faith, and, before entering the water, renounce the devil (obviously these are activities that infants can not perform).

In another reference to the *Martyr's Mirror*, Lesher points out that in the early church, people were baptized on their knees. While the mode of baptism is not mentioned, Lesher is certain that it was by a three-fold forward immersion, not one immersion backwards.[31]

Lesher also finds support for his views on baptism in radical Pietist Gottfried Arnold's *A Faithful Portrayal of the First Christians*. He characterizes this Lutheran scholar as a diligent scholar of the Bible. His knowledge of the Hebrew, Greek, and Latin languages (and possibly other languages) made him one of the most learned men of his time. Obviously Lesher thought highly of Arnold.[32]

In the passage that Lesher quotes, Arnold asserts that in the writings of the early church fathers, no mention is made of infant baptism in the first two Christian centuries. Anglican churchmen William Cave (1637-1713), a historian of the early church, and others could find no trace of infant baptism in these centuries.[33] Arnold concluded that no one was baptized except those who were growing into adulthood and knew the meaning of and prayed for the true baptism. Arnold referred to three church fathers (Walafrid Strabo [around 808-849], Basil the Great [around 330-379], and Hieronymian [around 342-420]) who all affirmed that the church practiced the baptism of believers. Arnold mentions that in the time of Cyprian (died 258) there was much discussion on whether infants were to be baptized on the second or eighth day of their birth. Such a controversy would not have occurred had infant baptism been a long established practice.

Lesher finds support for his views on immersion baptism in a German translation of Carl Buck's *Theological Dictionary*. According to this work, immersion baptism was and is the mode used by the Eastern and Greek Orthodox Churches. In the West, sprinkling was first introduced for people who were ill; sprinkling did not become the common practice until the fourteenth century.

Lesher ends by saying that he will write no more about baptism. He doubts that anyone can be persuaded of his position by further words, if they have not been persuaded by the information already given.

He moves to exploring the second statement, namely, that those who die before being baptized, such as infant children, will need to suffer through a painful purifying fire after death because of hereditary sin. Lesher says that these people believe they have a biblical basis for their view in Exodus 20:5, which states that God is a jealous God who will visit the "iniquity of the father upon the third and fourth generation." But Lesher asks his readers to read the next words: "of them that hate me." These are the people who say it is impossible to keep the commandments and walk in God's way, who see the laws as difficult and follow the way of sin as defined in 1 John 2:15,16: "the lust of the flesh, the lust of the eye and the pride of life" (one of Lesher's favorite verses defining the sinful life).

These people will be punished for their own sins, not those of their forefathers.

The next verse in Exodus 20 states that God will be merciful towards those who love him and keep his commandments. This, as well as Lamentations 5:7, Lesher insists, deals not with children but with adults who know the difference between good and evil and have the ability to do either one or the other. He also quotes Deuteronomy 24:16 and Jeremiah 31:28-30 to show that everyone shall die for their own sins. Lesher's conclusion is that God will not punish unknowing children for the sins of their parents.

The third belief that Lesher addresses is that the children of believing parents will be saved if they die before becoming aware of sin, while children of non-believers will be lost if they die before the age of accountability. Those who hold these views, Lesher indicates, see Romans 11:16 as foundational to their belief: "For if the first fruit be holy, the lump is also holy, and if the root is holy, so also are the branches.[34]

One must understand this verse in the context of the entire chapter, Lesher insists. Then it becomes clear that the chapter has nothing to do with innocent children born in the flesh, but with those born of the Spirit who have become God's children, grafted on to the holy root. That root is Jesus Christ, promised to Adam, Abraham, and David, the root of Jesse mentioned in Ruth and prophesied in Isaiah.

1 Corinthians 7:14, Lesher shows, is another verse used by those who support this third belief. That verse states that the unbelieving spouse is sanctified by the believing spouse, and ends with "else were your children unclean; but now are they holy." This verse, however, does not mean that one spouse will effect the other spouse's salvation, although a spouse could be the means of bringing the marriage partner to Christ as they pray together for each other or for their children. The greatest blessing and advantage believing parents can give their children in leading them toward salvation is to live devoted lives.

In summary, Lesher insists that no person can save or make holy another individual, for that is the work of God through Jesus Christ. He ends his refutation of the third belief by quoting (with some flexibility) biblical verses that underscore that all children have a sinful nature, and that Christ made provision for the salvation of all.

The fourth belief that Lesher evaluates through the "scales of holiness" is that children are saved through the merits, blood, and sacrifice of Jesus Christ. The starting point is an understanding of the nature and depth of original sin. To explore this question, attention must be given to Eve's sin in the garden. She made five mistakes: first, heeding the serpent's word that she would become wise; second, noting the beauty of the tree and edibility of the fruit; third, allowing the lust impulse to arise; four, eating the forbidden fruit; five, giving it to her husband. The result was the origin of sin, death, and lust within all posterity. Lust brings death, as James 1:14-15 reminds us. Given such a reality, Lesher warns his readers to be very careful (in this, quoting Rom. 7:5-7,18).

In writing of the spiritual state of children, he quotes Mark 10:14,15, which states that little children were to have freedom to come to Jesus, for of such is the kingdom of God. Those who refuse children this privilege will be denied entrance into the kingdom. Lesher repeats his earlier statements that all children have original sin, but they are not guilty of knowingly committing sin; thus God's gift of salvation is theirs without repentance and conversion. Jesus Christ has paid their debt of original sin. But once a child becomes aware of doing wrong, he or she becomes accountable and needs to repent, in support of which he quotes several passages.[35]

Lesher agreed with the Anabaptists and German Baptist Brethren that all children have a bent to sin, are free from original sin, and become accountable and guilty of sin when their consciences inform them that they are doing wrong. His use of Anabaptist and Pietist sources in this third chapter provides further evidence that he was aware of his historical roots. Believers conversion and baptism and church discipline were central to Anabaptism. The necessity of heart conversion, holy obedience, the corporate life of believers, and true faith issuing in true practice were part of the Pietism of the German Baptist Brethren.[36]

Chapter Four
Predestination and Human Freedom

In this last chapter (about one-half the length of the book), Lesher considers the doctrines of predestination and free will. In addition to seeking to refute Calvinistic predestination on biblical grounds, he gives attention to conversion, holiness and discipleship, and eschatology, largely as they relate to predestination.

This was a timely subject. During much of the nineteenth century, American Protestant Christianity was involved in the Arminian-Calvinist controversy, and during that time was moving toward Arminianism. Many Pennsylvania-Germans were either Lutheran and Reformed, thus often favorable to predestination. In Lesher's Chambersburg area, the Reformed papers, *Weekly Messenger* and *Kirchen-Zeitung*, carried articles on both free will and predestination. The articles indicate that these subjects were being discussed around Chambersburg. Very likely some Brethren in Christ read the articles, especially those who shared Lesher's opinions.[37]

Lesher begins with a historical survey. Prior to Augustine, there were churchmen who excessively emphasized human ability and works to secure salvation (Lesher does not mention Pelagius, widely reputed as holding such views). Augustine in the fifth century sought to correct this error by declaring that salvation was only by grace. Lesher quotes from Buck's *Dictionary* to show that in the fifth century some theologians went further by asserting that Christ did not die for all humankind (known as limited atonement); one's eternity is determined solely by God (unconditional election). Nothing could alter people's destiny—not Christ's suffering, correct doctrine, praying, fasting, or acts of charity.

In a preview of his position, Lesher sharply rejects such views as contrary to Scripture, which teaches that those who act, seek, and knock will be rewarded. But this affirmation appears to be somewhat at variance with his previously stated view that non-believers are spiritually dead.

Lesher quotes from Buck's *Dictionary* to explain John Calvin's position that the only reason for the eternal salvation of certain individuals is God's unconditional decree (not only his foreknowledge but also his will). Lesher insists that predestinationists have misinterpreted the verses of Scripture that they think establish their position. But his refutations are not always logically and systematically forged: his pastoral concern means that he wants to win hearts rather than debates.

Lesher does not see any problem with John 6:44,65 ("No man can come to me except the Father which hath sent me draw him"), because God's salutary grace "hath appeared to all men" (Titus 2:11), Christ is the "true light which lighteth" all humans (John 1:9), and God "wills that all men be saved" (1 Tim. 2:11). It is God who initiates an individual's salvation experience; humans ever so faintly are awakened and respond.[38]

Lesher explains his understanding of "free predestination" by reference to Romans 9:11-22. He believed that God's knowledge of how Jacob and Esau would respond was predetermined not by God's unconditional decree but on his omniscient wisdom which foresaw the kind of persons the two brothers would become.[39]

In a second illustration, Lesher shows that Pharaoh's hardened heart (Rom. 9:17) was due to God's raising up Pharaoh to show God's power and to make God's name known worldwide. This shows that no one can hinder God's power or keep him from punishing the wicked. At the same time God has mercy on those who have repentant hearts; he will have mercy on whom he will, and will harden the hearts of whom he will. This does not mean that God hardens peoples' hearts; rather, hearts begin to harden when they resist the grace of God and go their own way. Pharaoh's heart was hardened not by God's absolute will but by Pharaoh's own personal will.[40]

A third example Lesher uses is the potter and the control he has over his clay (Rom. 9:20-22; Isa. 30-12-14; Jer. 18:11). The first task of the potter is to find good clay; not all clay is usable for his work. The potter next works with the clay; if it is malleable, he places it on the wheel and goes to work. If he runs into problems, he will begin again. God moves in a similar way, giving people more opportunities to repent. Finally, the clay is refined by fire in the kiln. Defects may show in the final firing.

The point of the illustration is that the initiative toward salvation and holiness is with God. He searches for the right clay, molds it (repeatedly if necessary), and refines it with fire. Heaven is the end. God moves in love to save and sanctify. Humans respond by accepting God's provisions or rejecting them.[41]

In his refutation of Calvinism, Lesher next turns to Christ's parable of the workers in the vineyard, which ends with the words, "thus the last will be first, and the first last, for many are called but few chosen." The workers in the parable who were hired first and worked the longest wanted more pay than those hired later, although they had all agreed to the same wage. Lesher sees the workers hired first as representing the Jews of the Old Testament, who were called first, who received the law and the ordinances, and the promise that Christ would come. Their being called first is also seen in Paul and Barabas telling the Jews in Antioch that it was necessary to preach to them first, but since the Jews rejected the message, it was taken to the Gentiles. Lesher concludes that the last called (Gentiles) will be first in the new church, and the first called (Jews) will be the last.

This parable relates in Lesher's thinking to the parable of the wedding feast (Matt. 22:1-14), in which the king prepared a wedding feast for his son and sent out his servant to invite people to the wedding. Lesher refutes the interpretation offered by some that the kingdom in the parable is the eternal kingdom: it is not possible to force one's way into such a kingdom without the wedding garment. In similar fashion, some see the sheepfold of John 10:1-4 as the eternal kingdom, but no thief or robber would be allowed into the eternal kingdom. Lesher is convinced that in both cases the kingdom refers to the church. Since many join the "outer" church in some way other than through the true door (Jesus Christ), it can be said that many are called but few are chosen; many become church members but only a few belong to Christ. Lesher's interpretation of these parables reinforces his stance on the believers church.

Some people think, Lesher adds, that because the tables were full, those who came to the wedding feast were both good and bad people. But that is a wrong perception: all who came had to wear a wedding garment. For context, Lesher explained that in New Testament times, people did not make or buy their own wedding garment. Rather, they each received a garment as a gift from the king. The garments were all identical with the bridegroom's. Lesher draws the spiritual parallel: only the truly converted and committed receive the gift—the spiritual wedding garment.

Lesher wants his readers to be clear that it is not to be taken from the parables that unconverted, godless people are to be taken into the church. No intelligent person would read that the apostles and disciples taught this concept. True believers, Paul said, were "washed . . . sanctified . . . justified in the name of the Lord Jesus and by the spirit of Our God" (1 Cor. 6:10,11). It is possible that some can creep in unawares (Gal. 2:4), but when the bridegroom comes, the foolish virgins will be locked out. If the wicked were allowed into the banquet, there would be more wicked present than the good; it is surprising that only one wicked person is among the guests.[42]

Lesher insists that the reason only a few are chosen is not God's unconditional election of a few people and eternal damnation of the rest. Why would God call people to repentance if he did not want to save everyone? He sent his servants into the highways to invite all to come to the feast, and he commanded his disciples to go into all the world to preach the gospel.

Lesher considers the wearing of the wedding garment as putting on the Lord Jesus Christ (Rom. 13:14). Biblical examples of those having put on the garment and being taken into the church in the right way are Peter baptizing Cornelius and his group upon their receiving the Holy Spirit, and those to whom Paul writes as children of faith who have put on Christ (Gal. 3:26,27). Of course, the "chosen" need to continue in the faith to make their calling and election sure (2 Peter 1:5-10).[43]

Lesher is deeply concerned about the negative spiritual and moral effects of belief in predestination. There are people ready to repent of their sins and who hope for assurance of salvation, but when they do not readily receive the desired end, they may become discouraged and believe the tempting of the devil that they are not among the elect. In such a state, some have committed suicide. Other people, who do not sense their sinful nature, will reason that they are not among the elect, thus they may as well enjoy the pleasures of the world.

Then there are individuals who are so sure of their election that they do not truly repent. Instead they live frivolous lives, adorning themselves with the fashions of the world. Others believe that if they are among the elect, God will always call them back, even if they become involved in sin.

In short, Lesher asserts, Calvinistic predestination, with its doctrines of irresistible grace, total depravity, unconditional election, eternal security, and limited atonement subverts true evangelical faith. God can not be blamed if people go to hell; rather, he seeks the salvation of all people (Ezek. 18:21-23; 3:11; 1 Tim. 2:4; 2 Peter 2:9).[44]

Lesher clarifies his views by telling the story of a man who fell into a deep well. A friend came along who dropped the end of a rope to the man in the well, telling him to take the end of the rope so he could be drawn to safety. On his own, the man is helpless, but by willing to take hold of the rope (free will), he can be saved. "No man comes to me," Lesher quotes, "except the Father . . . draws him."[45]

Lesher issues a strong call for conversion. "Oh sinner," he writes, "leave your sins! Leave the broad way that leads to hell! Leave the lusts of the world and the flesh! Leave all pride and pomp and proud-mindedness and comparison [modeling after] the world! Leave all ungodly things, or you will be eternally lost! Begin to be modest, devout, just, pious, and live a holy life in this world, then you will live and die as a Christian."[46]

To sharpen his understanding of conversion, Lesher defines three false perceptions of conversion. One is built on the fear of death and hell, and the desire to go to heaven. A second kind is when so-called converted persons show no evidence of change in their lives.

A third kind of false conversion (identified as "short term") begins with "a lot of commotion and noise at the bench" (the context is a public revival meeting). Such conversions are mixed with many "unreal, impure and human activities and characteristics. . . . For the most of them, the best that can be said is that they are . . . an awakening from . . . the sleep of sin so that the individuals involved feel and see merely the necessity of a conversion." They think or pretend that they are converted, but they lack depth repentance, the receiving of the divine nature, and the crucifying of the flesh.

Yet Lesher is not willing to close the door on people who have this third kind of conversion. Such persons can be fully converted if they "will harbor within their hearts the quiet attention of the gentle appealing voice and the delightful drawing of God in the heart." Elijah heard the voice of God, not in the strong wind, earthquake, or fire, but in the still small voice.[47]

The purest and most genuine conversions "usually take place in the private [hidden] area of the human heart between God and the soul alone." That is the point made by Jesus when he told his disciples not to be like the hypocrites who pray openly on the street corners to be seen by men, or like the heathen who think they will be heard because of their many words. Rather, one is to enter into one's closet, close the door, and pray alone to God from the heart (Matt. 6:5,6,7). When the individual "persists in prayer and continues in secret prayer, and at other times is active in reverent worship toward God in his inner life and also in outward expression, it can lead the soul to a continual development of penitence. . . ."

Such true repentance does not depend on a fear of hell or on a selfish desire for heaven. Rather, through "a mature, tender [gnawing] conscience which makes us aware of our future destiny," there develops a "true sorrow of sin," which is always coupled with a love for God. With this comes "a hatred for self and a wholesome and basic self denial of all that is contrary [offensive] to our Lord God." The individual must give himself totally into the hands of God. Lesher calls for a total surrender, a complete openness to God.[48]

In such a heart there is evidence of "genuine evangelical repentance." If the soul maintains itself in this fashion and "clings to the Lord until the sweet soft sighing reveals . . . the Lord is inwardly present" (1 Kings 19:12), the soul will be filled and "endued with power from on high" (Luke 24:29). It will, in waiting, have its strength restored so that it will "go aloft like on the wings of eagles," running and walking but not tiring (Isa. 40:31). God's love will be poured into the heart by the Holy Spirit (Rom. 5:5) and the Spirit will testify with the human spirit that we are children of God (Rom. 8:16). The truly converted will give themselves fully to do what God wants. Having received a new nature, the newly-born will follow the guidance of the Holy Spirit and the example set by Jesus.[49]

Several aspects of Lesher's understanding of conversion merit further comment. His negative response to emotionally induced "short conversions" represents a rejection of public revivalism.

There was considerable opposition to such revivalism in such bodies as the Mennonites, German Baptist Brethren, Lutherans, and Reformed. Revivalism was well known in Franklin County and beyond. John W. Nevin, a professor at the German Reformed Seminary at Mercersburg located some twenty miles southwest of Chambersburg, was in sharp opposition to the movement. In an article, "The Anxious Bench," he characterized Charles Finney's revival activities as given to spurious emotionalism fostered by theatrical devices.[50]

Such opposition did not deter the revivalists. But 1810 camp meetings–bilingual and interdenominational—were held among the Pennsylvania Germans, attended by a variety of denominations, including some Brethren in Christ. The first all-German camp meeting, sponsored by the United Brethren, was held in August 1815 at Rocky Springs in Franklin County. Samuel Huber, a Mennonite who turned United Brethren preacher, wrote of the meetings: "Many sinners fall down, through the power of the word preached, as if dead, but rose again, shouting victory." In 1855 at John Snyder's place in Franklin County, meetings were held at which every night "old and young fell prostrate before the altar, crying for mercy." Clearly camp and revival meetings were a part of the Franklin County scene during Lesher's adult life.

In contrast, Lesher's understanding of conversion reflected a quiet, more inwardly intense experience, one that was of longer duration than that obtained in public revival meetings. When the Brethren in Christ accepted revivalism in the last decades of the nineteenth century, some were critical of the short and superficial nature of conversion experiences. Even when revivalism became generally accepted among the Brethren in Christ, the "mourner's bench" was not used, at the earliest, until the mid-1890s, in some places not until later.[51]

In introducing his discussion on holiness and obedience, Lesher closely relates holiness to the conversion experience: in both cases, humans have a choice to make—giving up one's will to do God's will. Intention is not enough: the holy life must be lived out in all actions, in exercising all virtues, all goodness. The qualities of goodness are like a chain: break one link and the whole becomes useless.

The link of modesty rules out all "immodest fault finding," a condemning spirit, and all meaningless talk. Moderation is to be practiced not only in speech but also in "eating, drinking, attire and in the use of all gifts of God." The "strict, domineering, impatient element" is to be denied in the interests of loving one another.

As Lesher has already indicated, foundational to holy living is the godly nature received in conversion. The godly nature is love. This love, among other things, is also brotherly love, for the Christian who loves God will also love all others born of God (1 John 5:1). But further, this is a general love that flows to all people, because God loves them and wants them to know the truth. The godly nature issues in godliness, which in turn leads to holiness. The end result is worshiping and serving God in "childlike fear . . . and childlike trust," fully resigning and subjecting oneself to doing God's holy will.

Lesher then proceeds to develop the biblical basis for godliness and holiness. Paul wrote: "Godliness is profitable unto all things," both in this world and the one to come (1 Tim. 4:8). Interpreting this verse, he says that although bodily exercise may be of little value, yet when essential, it can be of value as progress "in steps" toward holiness. Paul says of the Christians at Rome that before they knew Christ, they practiced "uncleanness from one degree of impurity to another." Paul now wants them to give themselves over to holiness degree by degree so that they "may become holy" (Rom. 6:19). Such persons will be called together when the last trumpet sounds. Paul also prayed that God would fully sanctify his readers and keep them safe and blameless until Christ's return (1 Thess. 5:13). Forget not to strive after holiness, Lesher emphasizes, for without it "no person will see God" (Heb. 12:14).

Lesher insists that holiness involves being separated from unbelievers. This does not mean separation from believers who belong to other, "external" fellowships. To have no contact with them would be a form of "sectarianism," which God sees as carnal (1 Cor. 1:12; 3:3), and goes against Jesus' repeated teachings that Christians are to love one another. Apostle John wrote that when Christians love one another, outsiders will know that they are disciples of Christ.

But Christians are not to mingle and be united with "unbelieving and unregenerate and unconverted people. Nor are they to be seen, unless it is necessary, in places where there is jesting and laughter." He quotes in full the six verses of 2 Corinthians 6:14-7:1 which repeatedly make the point of separation: light from darkness, righteousness from unrighteousness, Christ and Belial, etc. Those verses end with the words: "Go on to holiness in the fear of the Lord."

Lesher reiterates that the way of holiness is the way of love. God is love and anyone who loves God is in union with God in rejecting evil and doing good. One who knew the way of holiness, he informs his readers, was the pious Tobit of the Old Testament Apocrypha, who wrote, "Keep God before your eyes and in your heart," giving no place to sin and what is contrary to God's commands (Tob. 4:6). It is true, Lesher concedes, that in carrying out our human duties, we can not consciously meditate on God at all times, but what Tobit has in mind is that in all we do, we are to see ourselves as doing it in the presence of God. God surrounds us "like the atmosphere"; we "live and move and exist in him" (Matt. 5:34; Acts 7:28).

If one lives the life of love just described, love can sweeten the most bitter suffering." (It is not that one will always have a lively feeling of love, because feeling love and doing love at times are two different things.) God's love in our hearts enables us to live through discouragement and difficulties because we know that God allows such things in our lives for our purification and "to bring us to full sanctification." The Lord loves those whom he chastens (Prov. 3:11, 12; Heb. 12:5-8; Rev. 3:19). In short, love God, not the world.

Much of Lesher's writing on holiness has a Wesleyan ring. Owen Alderfer characterized the earlier Brethren in Christ understanding of holiness in much the same fashion as did Lesher, prior to the Brethren in Christ acceptance of the holiness doctrine.[52] Pietism and Wesleyanism, as is well documented, were both part of the experiential renewal movement in Western Christianity in the seventeenth and eighteenth centuries; both emphasized heart-centered faith, holy living, and moral earnestness.[53] It is understandable that the Brethren in Christ, as they moved from the German language to the English in the free American society, were open to Wesleyan understandings of the faith. Lesher makes no reference to a distinct second work of grace or that he attained to a sinless state, but his heart was committed to perfection.

For Lesher the life of love calls for daily devotions. On rising in the morning, dress out of a love for God, being aware that clothing is necessary because of the fall, and thankful that God instructed man how to make clothing (Gen. 3:21). Because of a love for God, have morning family devotions on your knees, thanking God for the night's rest and bodily health, and asking for the sense of his presence during the day. At mealtime, eat out of a love for God and, after asking his blessing on the food, partake not because the food is tasty but because it gives energy to do the work God has given you to do (Gen. 3:17-19). At the end of the day, again gather the family and on bended knee thank God for his blessing and ask him for protection and his love for the coming night. The Pietist movement made much of the devotional life because Pietists saw it as a means of fostering inner spirituality and holy living.[54]

Throughout his emphasis on always loving God, doing his will, and making a total surrender, Lesher explicitly and implicitly calls for complete self-denial. This includes having a humble spirit and living a lowly life (Rom. 12:16; Ecclus. 3:16 [Old Testament Apocrypha]). Be sure that you are not drawn to anything that you can not leave promptly if you learn that it is contrary to God's will. Be ready to do the will of others rather than your own, unless it is contrary to God's will.

In clothing, nothing is to be done out of vanity or glamor, and nothing is to be added that is "superfluous and unnecessary." The same holds true in "eating and drinking, in housing and home furnishing, in the use of animals with riding and traffic [driving]." Moderation is a good principle in all things.

Care is to be taken in using God's gifts to us (apparently he refers to earthly possessions). Some are tempted to say that this or that teaching doesn't apply to me, but God knows the condition of the heart. What is highly esteemed among men is an offense before God (Luke 16:15). Keep in mind the story of the rich man who dressed in purple and lived in luxury but who was tormented in hell (Luke 16:19, 23, 24).

A true Christian, Lesher maintains, will be ready for opposition. But hold fast, for opposition is the means of becoming stronger. By it we are purified, as gold and silver is by fire. Continually standing firm is the means to perfection, the means to a "genuine entry and transition into Jesus Christ."

The last subject that Lesher treats in his writing on predestination and free will is eschatology. He believes that the biblical revelation regarding last things supports his views on predestination and free will. The Bible calls for faithfulness and holiness to the end of life on earth.

An important aspect of American Christianity in the nineteenth century was millenialism. In general, postmillennialism was the predominant view held in the first part of the nineteenth century, premillennialism in the latter part. William Miller, a Baptist lay minister from New England, did much to popularize premillennialism. Millerism spread throughout south-central Pennsylvania, including Franklin County. Writing in 1849, Lesher was aware of these developments.[55]

Futurist Lesher reminds his readers that those who are "faithful unto death" will receive the crown of life (Rev. 2:10). To those people who say that few realize such a high level of holiness, Lesher answers that "many are called but few are chosen." Apostle Peter spoke of those who are refined by fire experiencing joy unspeakable and the salvation of their souls (1 Peter 2:0). Jesus said that on his return people will be rewarded according to their deeds (Matt. 16:27).

Lesher outlines the course of events at the end of time. Christ will return in the heavenly clouds, and, with the aid of his angels, will gather together the righteous who will be caught up in the clouds to meet him. The dead in Christ will be resurrected (the first resurrection), and together with the sanctified living will have their early bodies transformed into glorified spiritual bodies. The "old fleshly earth" will be destroyed by great heat (2 Peter 3:13), and be replaced by a "new glorified imperishable earth," as it was before the sin in Eden. On this new earth, Christ and his chosen ones will reign for a thousand years, and full righteousness will be a reality. At Christ's return, the ungodly will perish and Satan will be bound for one thousand years. Lesher saw the millennium as "an interval between time and eternity."[56]

Lesher sketches the glorious nature of the millennium. Those who have denied themselves, have separated themselves from the world, and have given no place to worldly lust will experience a thousand years of "paradisiacal peace and pleasure." In the millennium, "there is to be no form of contradiction, no duplicity, no self esteem, and no jealousy. . . . A holy accord and unity of thought will prevail, for here they will all be united in faith and in profession of trust in the Son of God (Eph. 4:13). Simplicity and a childlike manner will be the charm of their blessed existence; purity and love will be their mark of identification because divine and genuine love will possess their hearts and kindle in them the spiritual fire and all in this place will be fervently aglow."[57]

This description is a projection of the fully harmonious community populated entirely by sanctified, loving, and joyous saints. The inner and outer ideals and practices of Christians in the present life are fully actualized in the Kingdom of God.

Lesher follows his description with a five-stanza song (or poem), which he probably wrote. It calls for patience in our pilgrimage through life, and reflects a yearning for the coming Kingdom.

Oh come and hurry blessed times! Come soon and fill us with peace and joy! To live in these miserable circumstances is to die continually and to float about in desperation.

We live in suffering and lamentations on the earth, hoping that God will soon redeem us. Oh Lord Jesus come soon to give us joy! Come as a priest to consecrate us unto you!

We are pilgrims and strangers here. We can do nothing other than die and waste away. We are counted for little and see with horror how earthly wickedness cries to high heaven.

Nearly everything runs counter to your laws. The curse and evil chase the blessing away. Oh godly love we desire to have you, and if it is all right with you, we will take it even without many gifts.

We have given ourselves to you in life and death. Save us from evil and all corruption! We want to cling to you, even into death, not leaving you, regardless whether we live or die![58]

Like the foolish virgins, many will be locked out of the future Kingdom, not because of the absolute predestination of God, but because they have not cooperated with God's call or have not obtained the degree of holiness necessary to enter the Kingdom. Many were not willing to carry the likeness of Christ which involves self-denial and dying to self. Though living lives of outward decency, they remained complacent. These people may not have entirely gone over to Satan. They will spend the millennium in an intermediate state; they will be purified during the one thousand years. Though not suffering hellish pain, they will experience a "thousandfold gnawing and vexations about repentance," and will be frustrated because they did not give themselves entirely to God. In the postmillennium eternity, they will be "saved by fire," although not to the same degree of glory as the fully committed (1 Cor. 3:14-15; 15:41-42). It appears that Lesher envisioned a state similar to the Roman Catholic teaching on purgatory.

At the end of the thousand years, Satan will be let loose again for a short time. He will deceive the nations and gather a mighty army consisting of resurrected damned souls who lived in dark seclusion during the thousand years. Their effort to take the "holy beloved city" and to destroy the sanctified will be thwarted by God's wrathful fire falling on them from heaven.

After the devil is cast into the lake of fire, all humankind will be brought before the great white judgement seat. God will divide all people into two groups, the godly and the ungodly, the former to receive eternal life, the latter to be cast into the lake of fire, which will be the second death. (Lesher does not describe the nature of heaven here, but does so in his subsequent *The Spiritual Clockwork*.)

A better understanding of Lesher's millennium views may be gained by comparing them with those of William Miller, mentioned earlier. The two men were contemporaries, Lesher having been born only seven years before Miller (Lesher lived seven years longer). Frank Demmy has shown that both were largely premillennialists (Christ's return on clouds, a first resurrection, a thousand-year reign by Christ and true Christians, the apocalyptic conflict between Christ and Satan, the final judgement with Satan with the godless cast into the lake of fire, and the godly ushered into heaven).

But the differences in their views are clear. Miller gave considerable attention to the book of Daniel, whereas Lesher did not cite that or any other book in the Old Testament when discussing eschatology.[59] Miller became an evangelist, trying to save as many souls as possible before Christ's return, and set a time for it (1843-1844), which he had to revise to October 22, 1844, when the first date failed. His followers became Seventh Day Adventists. In contrast, Lesher did not set a date, and his evangelism was on a one-to-one basis.[60]

Understanding Brethren in Christ views on the millennium prior to the publication of *General Conference Minutes* (first published in 1871) and the beginning of the *Evangelical Visitor* (1887) is hindered because of lack of sources. The statement of belief of the founding fathers (around 1780) makes no mention of Christ's return, although no doubt they believed in the consummation of history with Christ's return. Christian Lesher gives the first known statement by Brethren in Christ of a thousand-year millennium.

Articles on the second coming began to appear in the *Evangelical Visitor* soon after publication began. In most cases the articles are written in an evangelistic manner—the reader should accept Christ in light of his imminent second coming. Some articles mention the millennium.[61] Enos Hess, president of Messiah Bible College (later Messiah College), wrote the first extensive explanation of the premillennial position in a series of ten articles published in the *Evangelical Visitor* in 1895 to 1896.[62] These articles were followed by nineteen by John R. Zook, who added a dispensational dividing of history.[63] Still other writers added other articles in the *Evangelical Visitor* to the now popular subject. A tract, commissioned by General Conference and first published in 1906, entitled "What We Believe and Why We Believe It," held strongly to premillennialism.[64] (The statement was revised in 1916 and in 1930.)[65]

For many years the premillennial position was widely taught, as well as preached by evangelists in revival meetings. Members in the West and Midwest were especially receptive to the teaching. In more recent years, little is heard among Brethren in Christ on the subject. It is not even mentioned in the most recent (2000) statement on Brethren in Christ core beliefs.

While the church was accepting premillennialism, they were also evaluating Millennial Dawnism, also known as Russellism after its founder, Charles Taze Russell. (The movement was the forerunner of the Jehovah's Witnesses.) Kansas members took the lead in condemning the movement in 1891, to be followed in the same year with the same action taken by General Conference. This did not entirely remove the problem, as in Kansas where the editor of the *Evangelical Visitor* was removed from his position when he began to show signs of being influenced by the movement, and as in Ohio where one congregation lost most of its members (including the pastor's wife) to Russellism.[66] But the influence of the movement on the Brethren in Christ eventually subsided, and since the 1920s it has not appeared to be a threat.

Conclusion

In *The Spiritual Magazine*, Christian Lesher ranges rather widely. Yet there is unity and direction in his thought. Jesus, being both divine and human is our Savior and Lord. As humans affected by the Adamic fall, we need a Savior; our human nature needs to be restored; we need to be brought into the fellowship of the church. Entrance to the church is by adult baptism, for only those who can truly believe can be part of Christ's body.

God's plan for human salvation is that all may be saved; salvation is not conditional and predetermined. Those who know Christ's love share it with others, in and out of the church. The church of the present will be fully actualized in the eternal kingdom.

NOTES

[1]The book was published by M. Kieffer and Company in Chambersburg, Pa. The English translation that I used is by Peter Hoover. The terms "Spiritual Storehouse" and "Witness to the Truth" indicate German Pietism's influence on Lesher. Another example of such usage was a religious periodical published by the

German Baptist Brethren leader, Christian Sauer II, in *Ein Geistliches Magazien*, published irregularly from 1764 to 1772. See *Brethren Encyclopedia*, s.v. "Geistliches Magazien," by Donald F. Durnbaugh, also Peter Erb, "Christian Lesher's 'Spiritual Magazine,'" *Brethren in Christ History and Life* (December 2000), 487-507.

[2]Interview with Jacob Sollenberger, June 6, 1989.

[3]*Spiritual Magazine*, p. 1; Erb, "'Spiritual Magazine,'" p. 488.

[4]*Spiritual Magazine*, p. 1.

[5]Letter of Noah Good to the author, September 20, 1989.

[6]Walter Klaasen, ed., *Anabaptism in Outline: Selected Primary Sources* (Scottdale, Pa.: Herald Press, 1981), pp. 23, 24; also Stoffer, *Brethren Doctrines*, p. 93.

[7]The docetic belief was condemned at the Council of Chalcedon (451) at which the church stated that Jesus Christ was "truly God and truly man." See *Evangelical Dictionary of Theology* (1984), s.v. "Docetism," by G.L. Borchert.

[8]*Spiritual Magazine*, chapter 2, p. 7.

[9]Ibid., chapter 2, p. 8.

[10]Ibid., pp. 8-10.

[11]Ibid., p. 9. Being dead did not mean an inability to respond as in Calvinistic predestination, but rather one could be spiritually lost and remain in that state throughout earthly existence, except in "sleepingly" hearing the message of salvation. See Manfred Kohl, *The Covenant Quarterly* (November 1974), pp. 15-25.

[12]Ibid., p. 10. The key expression in these translations in Genesis 1:24 and 2:19 is "living souls," in contrast to Luther's rendering of "living animals" (or living creatures). In addition, many early church fathers used the word "soul," not "animals."

[13]Letters of Noah Good to the author, September 20, 1989, and July 26, 1991; Peter C. Erb to author, September 24, 1992. The tripartite anthropology was commonly used by radical Pietists. See O'Malley, *Early German-American Evangelicalism*, p. 40.

[14]*Spiritiual Magazine*, pp. 10-11.

[15]Ibid., p. 12.

[16]Ibid., pp. 13-14.

[17]Ibid., pp. 14-16.

[18]Ibid., pp. 16-17.

[19]He quotes six passages: John 3:34; 2 Timothy 3:2-6; Ephesians 4:12-14; Hebrews 13:9; Romans 6:19; 1 Timothy 5:21.

[20]*Spiritual Magazine*, pp. 17-18.

[21]Ibid., pp. 18-19.

[22]Pietism strongly emphasized human sinfulness due to its roots in Luther and Calvin. Martin Schrag, "The Brethren in Christ Attitude Toward the 'World': A Historical Study of the Movement from Separation to an Increasing Acceptance of American Society" (Ph.D. diss., Temple University, 1967), pp. 26-31; *Dictionary of Christian Theology*, s.v. "Man, Doctrine of," by William Hordern; Luke L. Keefer, Jr., "Arminian Motifs in Anabaptist Heritage," in *Within the Perfection of Christ*, eds. Terry Brensinger and E. Morris Sider (Nappanee, Ind.: Evangel Press, 1990), p. 150; Klassen, ed., *Anabaptism in Outline*, pp. 41-42; *Mennonite Encyclopedia*,

Vol. 1, s.v. "Conversion," by S.F. Pannabecker and Vol. V, s.v. "Conversion," by George R. Brunk, III.

[23]*Evangelical Dictionary of Theology* (1984), s.v. "Dichotomy" and "Trichotomy," by W.E. Ward, and "Soul," by M.E. Osterhaven; *Encyclopedia of Early Christianity* (1990), s.v. "Soul," by Richard A. Norris; Stoffer, *Brethren Doctrines*, pp. 19, 30; Ensign, "Radical German Pietism," p. 326. Some present-day scholars point out that the Hebraic understanding is on the essential unity of humans, and that the belief in a two- or three-fold nature of man is rooted in Greek philosophy, not the Bible. See *Westminster Dictionary of Christian History*, s.v. "Soul," by Alan Richardson.

The concepts of dichotomy and trichotomy go back to Greek philosophers Plato and Aristotle, respectively. When Christian theology took shape in the first centuries, the intellectual world was dominated by Greek philosophy, with the result that views on dichotomy and trichotomy influenced Christian thought. Origen, an early church father, was a trichotomist. Both views became a part of Christian theology and were used by different theologians in different ways.

[24]L.P.D., "The Mode of Baptism," *Weekly Messenger*, October 6, 1841, p. 1258; W.C.B., "A Short Way with the Baptists," ibid., May 11, 1842, p. 1383; O.P.O., "Buried with Christ in Baptism," ibid., April 9, 1845, p. 1990; "Eingangs Rede der Disputation," *Kirchen-Zeitung*, July 15, 1853, p. 402; "Warnung gegen Ausgang aus die Kirche," ibid., March 15, 1851, p. 41; "Weider lin neues Buchlein," ibid., August 1, 1851, p. 114.

[25]*Spiritual Magazine*, chapter 3, p. 1.

[26]Ibid.

[27]Ibid. Menno Simon's work on baptism is available in John C. Wenger, ed., *The Complete Writings of Menno Simons*, trans., Leonard Verduin (Scottdale, Pa.: Herald Press, 1956), pp. 227-287.

[28]*Spiritual Magazine*, pp. 1-2.

[29]Ibid., pp. 2-3. The "scales of righteousness (or holiness)" refer to the inner heart transformed by grace being able to make evaluations of the spiritual life. With a new, God-given nature, discernment can be made about what is positive and what is negative in the Christian life. The basic point that Lesher is making in this passage is that there is no merit in simply going through an outer form, such as infant baptism. Involved is an ongoing reach for fuller holiness. Letter of J. Steven O'Malley to author, March 26, 2001.

[30]*Spiritual Magazine*, pp. 1-2. Letter of Noah Good to Schrag, September 20, 1989.

[31]As stated by Lesher, materials for his views on Tertullian were from the first part, page 104, of the *Mirror*. The same information is found in Thieleman J. van Braght, *The Bloody Theater or Martyrs Mirror*, trans. Joseph F. Sohm, 5th English ed. (Scottdale, Pa.: Herald Press, 1950), pp. 118-119. The second reference is identified by Lesher as being located on page 148 of his copy. Some of the material is found on page 157 of the 1950 edition.

[32]*Spiritual Magazine*, p. 3; letter of Good to Schrag.

[33]For Cave, see *The Dictionary of National Biography*, s.v. "Cave, William," by J.H.O. This church historian writes of the orientation of Arnold and Cave: "Arnold was influenced by William Cave's *Primitive Christianity* . . . but he reversed

Cave's evaluation. Whereas for Cave . . . the early church was a time of preparation for triumph with Constantine, for Arnold the unorganized and inspired earlier time was normative. Whereas Cave intended to restore the authority of the early councils and their creeds, Arnold located true religion among Jesus and the Apostles and Confessors before theologians took over Christianity." In Stoeffler, *Continental Pietism*, pp. 164-183.

[34]*Spiritual Magazine*, pp. 4-6. Letter of Noah Good to author.

[35]The passages are Romans 3:9-10; Galatians 3:22; 1 John 1:18; Acts 17:30; Luke 24:27; Colossians 1:14; Ephesians 1:7; Romans 3:24.

[36]Stoffer, *Brethren Doctrines*, pp. 27, 33, 66-69. The Berleburg Bible placed spirit and fire baptism as centrally important but it also had a place for water baptism. The writers favored a three-fold immersion baptism and stated that the person being baptized was to be an intelligent adult. At the same time the commentary writers differed in their theological perspectives. Those shaped by the Berleburg Bible were individualistic in respect to church patterns, especially as related to outer church structure and discipline. They were suspicious of "disciplined communities" and of corporately determined group life. Good letter to Schrag, August 12, 1991; William G. Willoughby, letters to Martin Schrag, May 20 and June 4, 1999; Ensign, "Radical German Pietism," p. 330.

[37]Sydney E. Ahlstrom, *A Religious History of the American People* (New Haven, Conn.: Yale University Press, 1972), p. 844; Edwin Scott Gaustad, *A Religious History of America* (New York: Harper and Row, 1966), pp. 144-153; *Dictionary of Christianity in America*, s.v. "Revivalism, Protestant," by W.G. Travis. For articles from the Reformed papers, see, "On the Perseverance of the Saints," *Weekly Messenger*, January 17, 1849, p. 2772; "Calvin's Limited Atonement," ibid., December 22, 1841, p. 1302; "Uber die Lehre von der Gnadenwahl," *Kirchen-Zeitung*, December 1852, p. 177; "Was ist unter 'Calvinism' zu Verstehen," ibid., February 16, 1852, p. 28; "Der Calvinismus des Apostels Paulus Bekehrung," ibid., April 10, 1852, p. 57. I owe assistance in using this material to Diana L. Rimert of the Evangelical and Reformed Historical Society in a letter to the author of January 3, 2001.

[38]*Spiritual Magazine*, chapter 4, pp. 2-3.

[39]Ibid., pp. 3, 4, 7.

[40]Ibid., pp. 8-9.

[41]Ibid., p. 10. Lesher's understanding of God's sovereignty and human freedom is more fully grasped when seen in the context of Calvinistic predestination. In the first Great Awakening (around 1735-1743), evangelist George Whitefield and theologian Jonathan Edwards preached and wrote that "salvation belonged completely to God and that humans did not possess the natural capacity to turn to Christ apart from God's saving call." Lesher believed that God initiated the relationship; humans in response can accept or reject the relationship. In the Whitefield-Edwards situation, the heart was warmed; it was an experiential experience entirely done by God. In the second Great Awakening (around 1795-1830), leaders such as Nathaniel Taylor believed humans always possessed a "power to the contrary." The change was away from Calvinistic predestination toward Arminian views of free will. Methodism re-enforced the move toward free will. See, *Evangelical Dictionary of Theology*, s.v. "Great Awakenings," by M.A. Noll, and

s.v. "Revivalism," by M.E. Dieter.

[42]*Spiritual Magazine*, pp. 12-13. See Good letter to author, September 20, 1989.

[43]*Spiritual Magazine*, pp. 15-17.

[44]Ibid., pp. 4, 5, 17, 18.

[45]Ibid., pp. 5-7. Lesher's concern about predestination was that it undercut the quest for holiness. He does not deal with the supralapsarian-infralapsarian debate; he must have considered them unbiblical. *Evangelical Dictionary of Theology*, s.v. "Predestination," by W.S. Reid, and s.v. "Elect, Election," by F.H. Klooster.

[46]*Spiritual Magazine*, pp. 18-19.

[47]Ibid.; Peter C. Erb letter to author, January 31, 1990.

[48]*Spiritual Magazine*, p. 18.

[49]Ibid., pp. 25, 26, 27.

[50]Don Yoder, "The Bench Versus the Catechism: Revivalism and Pennsylvania's Lutheran and Reformed Churches," *Pennsylvania Folklife* (Fall 1959), pp. 14-23. Yoder indicates that the Lutherans and Reformed reacted to revivalism in a sequence of three ways, the three happening in sequence. See also the same author's *Pennsylvania's Spirituals* (Lancaster, Pa.: Pennsylvania Folklife Society, 1961), pp. 41-46.

Other sources on revivalism include the following. *Mennonite Encyclopedia*, Vol. IV, s.v. "Revival," by Harold S. Bender, and Stoffer, *Brethren Doctrine*, p. 111. See also John Denig, ed., *Autobiography of the Rev. Samuel Huber, Elder in the Church of the United Brethren* (Chambersburg, Pa.: M. Kieffer and Co., 1858), pp. 37, 38, 120, 121, and "The Anxious Bench," in Edwin Scott Gaustad, ed., *Religious Issues in American Christianity* (New York: Harper and Row, 1968), pp. 118-130. John Nevin wrote: "Spurious excitements are natural and common. Gross irregularity and extravagance, carried often to the point of downright profanity, are actually at work, in connection with such excitements, on all sides" (p. 123 of Gaustad). "Very many thus introduced into the Church show too plainly, by their hallowed tempers, and the general worldliness of their walk and conversation, that they have never known what religion means" (p. 130). The German Reformed paper *Weekly Messenger* kept its readers informed about revivalism. See, for example, "The Anxious Bench, No. 1," January 24, 1844, and J.W.N., "The Anxious Bench, No. 2," January 31, 1844.

[51]Wittlinger, *Quest for Piety and Obedience*, pp. 9-12, 201-226; Alderfer, "The Mind of the Brethren in Christ," pp. 100-108.

[52]Alderfer, "The Mind of the Brethren," pp. 120-125; Sider, *The Brethren in Christ in Canada*, pp. 122-133.

[53]Theodore Tappert, "Introduction," in *Pia Desideria*, pp. 1-2.

[54]*Spiritual Magazine*, pp. 22, 23.

[55]George M. Marsden, *Fundamentalism and American Culture* (New York: Oxford University Press, 1980), pp. 48-55; Ahlstrom, *Religious History of the American People*, pp. 478-481; *Dictionary of Christianity in America*, s.v. "Miller, William," by G. Land; Frank Linn Demmy, "A Comparison of Premillennial View of Christian Lesher with the Teachings of Millerite Adventism" (unpublished term paper, Messiah College, 1972), pp. 2-10; "The Millennium," *Repository and Whig*, January 19, 1843. This last source was published in Chambersburg. "The

Millennium" was a sermon preached in Chambersburg. In the March 11, 1843 issue the editor reports receiving a book dealing with millennialism. The editor himself was opposed to Millerism.

[56]*Spiritual Magazine*, p. 25.

[57]Ibid., p. 27.

[58]Ibid., p. 27.

[59]Lesher, however, does cite 4 Ezra 7:26, a writing related to the Old Testament (the book is also referred to as 4 Esdras) thought to have been written after the fall of Jerusalem, and dealing with problems arising out of the destruction of Jerusalem. The work is included in the Apocrypha of the Church of England. Why Lesher used it is not known. For explanations of the book, see *Anchor Dictionary of the Bible*, s.v. "Esdras, Second Book of," by Michael E. Stone, and "Millennium," by J. Massyngbaerde Ford; *International Standard Bible Encyclopedia*, s.v. "Esdras, Books of," by R.A. Stewart; *Evangelical Dictionary of Theology*, s.v. "Adventism," by M.E. Dieter.

[60]Demmy, "A Comparison of Premillennial View of Christian Lesher," pp. 12-15; *Dictionary of Christianity in America*, s.v. "Miller, William," by G. Land; *Evangelical Dictionary of Theology*, s.v. "Millennium, Views of," by R.G. Clouse, and "Adventism," M.E. Dieter; Mark A. Noll, *A History of Christianity in the United States and Canada* (Grand Rapids: Eerdmans Publishing Co., 1992), p. 193.

[61]See articles in the *Evangelical Visitor* by Charles Baker, N.A. Engle, Mazie Hess, W.H. Eisenhower, and Elias M. Smith, from 1888-1892.

[62]The series by Enos Hess begins in the November 15, 1895 issue of the *Evangelical Visitor* and ends with the May 1, 1896 issue.

[63]The series by John R. Zook begins on the October 1, 1899 issue, and ends with the October 1, 1900 issue.

[64]*General Conference Minutes*, 1906, pp. 10,11. A copy of "What We Believe and Why We Believe It," is in the Brethren in Christ Historical Library and Archives. The statement on the second coming in the latter reads: ". . . We believe in the general resurrection of the dead, both just and unjust (Luke 14:14; Jno. 5:28,29; Acts 24:15; II. Cor. 5:10; Dan. 12:2); that the just shall rise at the second appearing of Christ, and be caught away from the earth (with the living saints) until it is purified by fire (I. Thess. 4:14-18; II. Pet. 5:9-13) that the unsaved at the same time shall be destroyed from the face of the earth (Ma. 4:1,2,3; II. Thess. 1:7-10; Matt. 13:37-42); that the saints shall reign a thousand years with Christ on the new earth in their glorified bodies (Matt. 13:43; II. Pet. 3:13,14; Heb. 1:10,11,12; Rev. 20:4,6; Dan. 2:44,45; 7:14 and 18 and 27); that the unjust shall be resurrected at the close of the millennium, and receive eternal punishment (Rev. 20:5,13,14,15; 21:8; Jude 7; Rev. 14:10,11; Matt. 10:28; 25:41); that the devil, sin, death, and hell shall also ultimately be cast into the lake of fire (Rev. 20:10, and 14; Matt. 13:14)."

[65]See the Manual of *Doctrine and Government* for those years.

[66]Wittlinger, *Quest for Piety and Obedience*, pp. 155-158; *Evangelical Visitor*, June 26, 1911, p. 4; ibid., September 26, 1911, p. 3; ibid., October 16, p. 3.

The Spiritual Clockwork
as a Witness to the Truth

In 1965, I found an eighty-page manuscript in German among the Christian Lesher papers in the Kittochtinny Historical Society Museum, Chambersburg, Pennsylvania. The document was translated by Noah Good under the above English title. To date no evidence has emerged to indicate that the work was ever published. Lesher was seventy-five years of age in 1850 when he penned the introduction.[1]

The use of twelve hours of the clock was not uncommon in the Pietist tradition.[2] The following examples from three writers illustrate the approach. Daniel Schuhmacher was the pastor of several Lutheran congregations in Berks and Lehigh Counties, Pennsylvania (around 1775); Andreas B. Bauer was reportedly a Mennonite in 1833.[3]

Schuhmacher	Bauer	Lesher
1. One thing necessary: to know Jesus Christ	1. One thing necessary: have faith in Christ	1. One God
2. Two ways: go the narrow way	2. Only two ways to go	2. Two testaments
3. Honor the trinity	3. Consider three: redemption, creation, sanctification	3. Trinity

4. Four soils (parable of sower) prepare your heart	4. Four last things: death, judgment, heaven, hell	4. Four animals (Rev. 4:7)
5. Five virgins: wedding feast	5. Five wounds of Jesus	5. Five human senses: ear, eye, nose, mouth, feeling
6. God's six days of creation	6. Six water jugs: wedding at Cana	6. God's six days of Creation
7. Jesus' seven words on cross	7. Jacob served seven years for Rachel	7. Seven spirits of God and seven spirits of Satan
8. Only eight souls believed in God	8. Eight souls saved in Noah's ark	8. Eight human emotions: love, hate, etc.
9. Nine lepers remained thankless	9. Redeemer accused in the winter (ninth) hour	9. Nine beatitudes
10. Ten pious people not found at Sodom	10. Ten virgins met bridegroom	10. Ten virgins met bridegroom
11. Christ spoke only to eleven before he went to garden	11. At eleventh hour master sent out workers– vineyard	11. At eleventh hour master sent out workers– vineyard
12. Who might die in today's twelve hours?	12. New Jerusalem has twelve gates of pearls	12. Number twelve in book of Revelation

Although these short statements somewhat obscure the point, it is possible to see that the three men sought to further practical heart-centered piety. The point of departure for all three writers was numbers. The numbers directly relate to biblical material, with only a few exceptions (primarily when Lesher deals with human senses and emotions). The spiritual instruction is well within the boundaries of Pietism. That a Lutheran, Mennonite, and Brethren in Christ should write in approximately parallel fashion illustrates the widespread influence of Pietism.

The use of numbers as a means to enrich spiritual vitality has a long tradition, going back to at least ancient Babylon. The use was expanded and systematized by some Greek philosophers (especially Pythagoras), Jewish scholars (such as Phila), and Gnosticism. The early church fathers were gradually influenced by this approach, and Augustine's use of the method opened the way for its wide use in Medieval times. Some mystics were drawn to numerology in their search for hidden or deeper meanings.[4] Understandably, the individualism of radical Pietism would have been fertile soil for mystical meaning in numbers.

Numbers have been used in a variety of ways to interpret religious experience. The three men noted above largely used numbers as a way of presenting truth in an enriching and easily remembered way. Numbers are also used symbolically, figuratively, and typically. When employed in this way, they are often identified with general concepts, for example, the number seven standing for completeness, the number one for unity. In the mystical use of numbers, there is a hidden, or secret, meaning in the number.

Much speculation has been given to the meaning of the number 153, the number of fish Simon Peter caught, as recorded in John 21:11. It has been suggested that 153 is the triangular number of 17 (153 is the result of adding 1+2+3+4, on up to 17). St. Augustine thought that 17 was a symbol of the gospel (law = 10 + spirit - 7).[5] Another method of mystical numerology is to assign numbers to letters (e.g., A=1, B=2, etc.). By using this method, the number 666 for the beast in Revelation (13:18) has been given to such people as the Roman Caesar Nero and the German Kaiser Wilhelm.[6]

Another aspect of numerology found in some systems is the belief that God created the world according to numerical and symmetrical design or pattern. This means that insight into reality can be gained by a careful study of the numerological phenomena of religion and nature, since the two are harmonious. For example, Jacob Boehme believed a trinitarian design was basic to both God and the universe.[7] The method can be extended to relate numbers to fire, sulphur, colors, metals, and stones.[8] The degree to which numerology has been taken shows Lesher to have been moderate in his use of the concept.

The Spiritual Clockwork is more devotional in nature than The Spiritual Magazine, although in it he continues to elaborate his theology. Some spiritual progression occurs in the work in that each chapter adds additional information on God's redemptive plan, with the last chapter climatically highlighting the New Jerusalem.

In the preface, in which he gives the rationale for his work, Lesher says that although there are many good Christian edificatory books, many of them are not readily available. Other books are too large, cover too many subjects, or are not written at the needed level of understanding. Furthermore, different people have different needs, and the needs of individuals vary from time to time. Lesher takes a cue from nature by saying that just as God reveals his truth through a rich variety of nature, he can do so also through a variety of writings.

The author explains that when he started to write, it was only for his personal benefit. He intended to write maybe a half page for each hour of the day. But he soon came to realize, through the urging of the Spirit, that God had a wider purpose or wider audience for his writing. He ends the preface by affirming the biblical nature of his writing, even though at times he may not be able to support all his statements with specific Bible texts.

One O'clock

In identifying the number one with God, Lesher stood in a long Christian tradition. He begins his discussion by pointing out that God is a spirit who is to be worshiped in "spirit and truth" (John 4:24). God is beyond comparison with any other god. He transcends human comprehension. In a heart-warming fashion, Lesher magnifies God's greatness, especially as this relates to his work with humans: "[God is] a good being that is above all else that is good; a Light that is the richest, purest, and brightest of all lights; a Power that is the mightiest of all and who is almighty; a Holiness that is beyond expression in words; a Passion which when compared with all other passions makes them merely clay or filth; a Source of joy which is far beyond all comprehension or understanding; a Love which [is divine] for God Himself is love; and a person who continues in love continues in God and God in him" (John 4:8-16).[9]

From this poetic expression, Lesher goes on to identify God as all knowing, everywhere present and immanent in all things, perfect in justice toward unrepentant sinners. He ends by claiming that there is no need to do any further research on the origin of God.

To illustrate, he tells the story that he once read in an "old writing." A man determined to learn the how and where of God's origin. In his travels he came to an ocean where he saw a boy who, wanting to find the source of the water, tried to empty the ocean by pouring water with a dipper from the ocean into a hole he had dug. When the man told the boy that the goal was beyond his reach, the boy replied that if the source of the visible ocean can not be found, certainly the search for the origin and nature of the invisible God was all the more fruitless. With that comment, the boy became an angel of God and ascended into heaven. The point is that God is unique. As transcendent, he comes to humans, rather than humans finding God.

Lesher mentions the trinitarian nature of the Godhead, then relates God's nature to God's work in creation, including righteous angels in the "blessed kingdom of heaven." This was a place of complete harmony with everything attuned to God's will until Lucifer, out of pride and the desire to be God, brought about hatred, violence, division, and jealousy. To retain heavenly unity God cast Lucifer out of heaven; since then Lucifer has been the source of all evil, including the fall from Eden and death. The remaining holy angels, deeply grieved by what Lucifer had done, remained faithful during a time of probation, with the result that since that time angels cannot be touched by temptation or sin. With the fall of the devil, God in his great wisdom and justice created the second kingdom—hell, the destiny of the devil and his followers.

In his omniscience, God saw that it would be good to create human beings who would take the place in heaven of the fallen angels. For this he created a third kingdom, the "kingdom of this earth," which he pronounced to be "very good." He placed man and woman in a wonderful garden, after populating this kingdom with all kinds of creatures for their use, and gave them the task of bringing into being a vast number of holy people, all made in the image of God. If humans had passed the probation test, they would have replaced the fallen angels and would have been in the state of holy angels, beyond temptation and sin.

Lesher claims that the period of probation was forty days. Adam and Eve did not know the length of this probation, otherwise they would have been obedient out of self-love, not out of total surrender to and pure love for God. He arrives at this precise time span on the basis of three subsequent crucial probation periods in the biblical revelation. The first probation came when God tested his people at Mount Sinai. God promised to make the Israelites a holy people if they would obey his law, his commandments. But when they failed by fashioning the golden calf during the forty days Moses was on the mountain, God could not write the law in their hearts and given them his Spirit.

The failures of Adam and Eve and the children of Israel were reversed by Jesus Christ. He also had to be tested; he proved faithful in the forty days in which he was tempted by the devil. Because of Jesus' victory through obedience, the law could be written in the human heart and the Spirit could dwell in that heart. (No mention is made of a third probation in the photocopy of the original German manuscript, but that may be owing to a page missing in the copy.)

Lesher moves from the effect of the fall to the solution for the sin condition, namely, the new birth and the new community in the next chapter. In this chapter, we have Lesher's most extensive consideration of the nature of God. He does not stay away from rational categories, but it is clear that in keeping with his heritage, the center of his concern is that God made provision for humans to know God experientially and to follow him in holy discipleship.

Lesher's belief in three separately created worlds and the several times of probation are hardly biblical; such concepts may have come from the Behmenist tradition.[10] At the same time, they did not alter his basic theological and experiential orientation.

Two O'clock

In this chapter, Lesher focuses on the law (Old Testament) and grace (New Testament). For him, law and grace are two basic components of the new birth. The result is that in chapter two Lesher provides his most extensive exposition of the new birth.

The law by its precision and pointedness makes one aware of "the lust to sin" (Exod. 20:17), but also of the holy righteousness of God. The sinner knows that he must leave sin but finds himself enslaved to it. Death and hell loom. In the Old Testament a "legal atonement" was available, but no other means.

In the new covenant, what the law could not do, Christ could. Coming in the form of sinful flesh, he condemned what the law condemned as sin in the flesh, so that the righteousness demanded by the law could be accomplished for us (Rom. 8:3-4). The law was a schoolmaster pointing us to Christ; it has within itself "light and illumination."

When there is a broken heart, God draws the broken spirit to him. He forgives the sinner and liberates him from sin slavery. The newly born rejoices in God-given joy, the restoration of the divine nature and the assurance of salvation.

Lesher's explanation of the role played by law is reminiscent of and was influenced by Luther's understanding of the law. His counsel regarding certain types of conversion relate to the accents of Pietism; the receiving of the new nature and the need and ability to walk in the footsteps of Jesus reflect both Pietist and Anabaptist influences.

Three O'clock

The number three leads Lesher to consider the Holy Trinity of God. He asserts that, although humans have difficulty understanding how three can be one, Scripture is clear on the triune God (Father,

Son, and Holy Ghost) being one (John 1:14). The triune nature of God is evidenced in creation, as seen in the words: "Let *us* make man." It is also evidenced in humans, made in the image of God and tripartite—body, soul, and spirit (1 Thess. 5:23). He shows how the three parts of humans are related to each other in the sinner and how conversion alters the relationship of the three.

Further evidence of the trinitarian nature of God is shown in the baptism of Jesus: the Father spoke from above, the Son was baptized, and the Spirit descended on the Son in the form of a dove. This three-fold action is the basis for baptizing in the name of the Father, Son, and Holy Ghost.

Lesher next explains the inter-relatedness of the three persons within the Godhead and how the work of three results in one person's salvation. He emphasizes that the Father and the Son are one ("I am in the Father and the Father in me"), and that the work and revelation of the Son is also the work of the Father. The Father and the Son sent the Holy Spirit to be the Comforter, teach all things, administer the work of Christ, and verify the oneness and integrity of the trinitarian nature of the one God.

In summary, since God is triune, he makes himself known and carries out the plan of salvation in a three-fold manner. The three in complete harmony carry out *one* plan of salvation.

Four O'clock

Lesher relates the number four to the four animals or beasts (he prefers the Berleburg Bible translation of "four living creatures") around the throne of God (Rev. 4:6,7) and to what he refers to as the four complexions or races of humankind. He sees the four creatures as central in God's revelation because of their close proximity to God. They are the "strongest, mightiest, the closest and most intimate in the counsel of God," and the first to know God's will. In addition, they have knowledge of both the past and future happenings ("eyes in front and behind"), and they have some influence on the course of events. More importantly, the features of the four creatures may have something to teach humans because the features represent the characteristics of the born again person.

Some "old writers," Lesher continues, believed that the four elements of human existence—fire, water, air, and earth—as well as the four races of humanity arose from the four creatures. The four angels are also involved in this creation process (the reference is perhaps to the four angels located at the four corners of the earth in Rev. 7:1). In referring to "old writers," he may have had in mind such Greek philosophers as Plato who believed that all elements and objects in the world are made up of the elements that Lesher cites. Such a Greek philosopher as Hippocrates defined humankind in terms of four complexions (races), as did some early church fathers.[11]

[Several pages are missing in Schrag's manuscript, apparently on the four animals relating to the four stages of life. Schrag's description of this chapter begins again with an explanation of Lesher's views of the four complexions.]

The first is the "choleric complexion," coming from the element of fire, characterized by a "willful and fiery nature and quick temperament," manifested in a "hot [and] . . . irritable . . . disposition." Such persons tend to be vigorous, "self-willed, overbearing, proud, bossy, and angry." Given their quick temper, they may kill someone without realizing that they are in a rage. Even after conversion, this nature tends to remain, causing conflicts with other people. They need to be careful not to be overtaken by fiery urges and do things they will later regret.

People who have a "sanguinary" complexion, related to air, have a "moderate . . . and steady temperament," a "loving, friendly and attractive nature," and a "penetrating intelligence." Usually "happy . . . and easy going," they need to guard against frivolity because this characteristic could lead them astray. They are understandably popular, thus they need to shy away from seeking the praises of people in favor of fearing God. When they encounter difficulties, they are not overly concerned because they are positive about the future, moving "just like the air that easily goes over anything in its path." Given the absence of an evil background and their happy nature, they have difficulty in truly repenting and entering into godly sorrow, unless God leads them to great spiritual difficulties.

The third type, the "phlegmatic" complexion, is related to water. People with this complexion are "feeble in intelligence," and have a "yielding and slow temperament." They are satisfied with almost anything, are "idle, lazy and drowsy," not easily taught, and unhappy about thinking through issues. Such people are not readily made sorrowful or anxious, yet at the same time they tend not be "cheerful" or "happy." Like water, they just flow along, easily shifted into another course, and easily "made cloudy." The result is that they are led astray and subject to temptation. Given their "cold, idle, indifferent and unconcerned" attitude, they cannot become serious about true repentance, and they do not have the will to "fight the fight of faith with zeal" to achieve spiritual victory. Understandably, many lapse into their old ways.

The fourth complexion, related to earth, is melancholy. As is true of earth, melancholy people have a "dark, cold, and shadowy temperament," resulting in a disposition that is fearful, doubting, and very uncertain in making decisions. They have a "profound understanding," and are not lazy or idle, but given their disposition, they are tempted to see disasters ahead. Cheerful when all is well, they are more often sad; they become downhearted when their feelings are hurt. At times they become "irritable and vengeful," while at other times by hiding their feelings, they are "useful, industrious, and thrifty."

Their conversion is hindered by their earthly temperament, which gives Satan the opportunity to make them feel uncertain and unable to have heart faith. The Evil One comes at them with unbelief and doubt, which leads them to think that there is no grace for them. In despair, some have committed suicide. In the spirit of a compassionate counselor, Lesher appeals to them: "I would like to urge you and advise, my dear soul, do not lose faith even if your situation would be even ten times more distressing, for indeed the enemy is too strong for you, but the Savior is so very strong! Let Him lead . . . you, he can do what no human can do. He breaks the strongest bond and brings rest to your state of life."

Melancholy persons should take courage, humble themselves, and think, "I shall not fail to draw nigh to God and to pray to Him, and . . . if I will be lost I want to be lost in prayer." Where there is genuine repentance, a will resigned to God's will, and a trusting spirit toward God, Satan will flee and God will come near.

In this chapter, the number (four) is more central than the numbers in the previous three chapters. There is more inherent or more commonplace religious connection between the number one with God, number two with the two testaments, and number three with the Trinity. That is, in these three combinations, the spiritual or devotional weight fall on God, the Testaments, and the Trinity. The continuity of the pattern can be seen in relating the four animals to the four states in the Christian life (although the Bible and orthodox Christian theology make more of combining one with God, two with the Testaments, and three with the Trinity).

But the continuity is broken by identifying four elements and four complexions with the Christian life. These elements and complexions are not drawn from Scripture; rather, they have their roots in Greek thought. (It is true that these classifications were made a part of Christian theology in some theological systems.) In this respect, it is significant that Lesher uses only three biblical references and that all three are at the end as he summarizes his thoughts.

There is nothing amiss in Lesher's use of the four elements and four complexions to gain insight into the Christian life. The point is that this illustrates how, within mysticism and radical Pietism, many foursomes were brought together mainly for the use of numbers. The categories of four elements and four complexions were rather commonplace in radical Pietism, which held that supernatural revelation was not limited to the biblical canon (as indicated in the Berleburg Bible) and that humans are a microcosm of the macrocosmic world.[12]

Five O'clock

Lesher relates the number five to the five human senses: hearing (ear), seeing (eye), smelling (nose), tasting (mouth), feeling (body). These five senses are a means of gaining greater insight into spiritual realities and of enriching the Christian faith.

Lesher reasons that since God created humans in a three-fold manner (spirit, soul, and body), each of the five senses may be considered in a three-fold manner; that is, each of the five senses spiritually understood may be related to each of the major aspects of humans—spirit, body, and soul.

His approach may be illustrated in his discussion of the soul, which, he claims, has five qualities: identification, thought/imagination, reason/memory, desire/longing, and change. These five qualities are only doors or windows through which the soul observes and understands outside influences.

To illustrate how humans use the five senses, he explains his understanding of how they discern color. This discernment comes in five stages: recognition and distinctions of color; determination of which colors are most appealing, recollection of what and why given colors were used in the past, the desirability of one color over the others, and appropriating one color over the other. (He takes the same approach to music.)

Lesher ends this chapter by explaining the nature of repentance and personal salvation in terms of the five senses, spiritually interpreted. The awakened conscience *hears* the quiet voice of God. Sin becomes very offensive, and the sinner sees that he is on the broad road that leads to destruction. The *smell* of sin becomes too much to bear (Ps. 38:4-7). The sinful things that once *tasted* good now become despicable. Finally, the sinner *feels* pain, fright, and a crushing sadness. This leads to godly sorrow and repentance. The soul now pleads for forgiveness and a pure heart (Ps. 6:4,8; 2 Cor. 7:10).

To the repentant person, God's grace effects forgiveness of sins and reveals the five spiritual senses. Spiritual *hearing* in the inner being means experiencing the "comfort and joy of the Holy Spirit," and knowing that one is at "peace with God" (Rom. 5:1). The newly born Christian *sees* the reality of such things as the grace, love, and goodness of God, and desires others to have the same blessing. The godly sense of *smell* comes alive and the Christian breathes the fragrance of sweet spices and ointments, and becomes a "sweet incense of Christ." When the sense of taste is Spirit-activated, nothing *tastes* better than the water of eternal life, the meat that does not perish, and the bread of eternal life (John 6:27,48,50,51). The person born from above *feels* pervading joy, and can say, "I rejoice in the Lord, and my soul is happy in my God . . ." (Isa. 61:10).

This use of the five senses and qualities of the soul to gain new insight into reality was fairly common to radical Pietism.[13]

Six O'clock

In this chapter, Lesher considers the six days of creation. As in the previous chapter, he shows that the physical universe points to and has continuity with the spiritual world; the two were created on the same pattern and for the same end. All of creation, Lesher states, is a reflection of God's image as the various days of creation show.

On the first day, in keeping with his nature and purpose, God created light. He next separated light from darkness; he calls for the same separation from darkness when he gives light to human hearts (2 Cor. 4:6). The light is not Christ himself, but it leads people to Jesus Christ. The light is revealed through God's grace appearing to all people. The more place we give to and the more fully we follow the light, the more separation from darkness will occur in our lives.

On the second day, God created a firmament by dividing the waters above from the waters below. Spiritually considered, the water above the firmament is godly wisdom, the water under it is earthly wisdom. Earthly wisdom, which is "carnal and devilish," is to be separated from, not confused with, spiritual wisdom, which is "chaste . . . peaceable . . . gentle, easily entreated, full of mercy and good fruits . . . and without hypocrisy" (James 3:15,17).

A danger of earthly wisdom lies in its shaping a Christianity that requires less self-denial and allows for a lower level of commitment. Such wisdom must be used in moderation, in order for us to live honorably in the present physical aspect of life. When the temporal part of life is kept in second place, God will allow more heavenly wisdom to flow into our lives.

God's creative act of the third day was to gather the water into seas, form dry land, and provide vegetation to make the land fruitful. Central to that fruitfulness would be humans, yet to be created. Their fruitfulness is to bring forth the fruits of the Spirit.

On the fourth day, God created the great lights, the large one to rule by day, the lesser by night. An orderly universe was now in place (seasons, days, and years). In the "new creation," Jesus Christ is the greater light, the "illuminated soul" (the converted person) the lesser light, which has no godly light in itself but reflects Jesus Christ, thus becoming the means of Christ's light shining in the world. The changing phases of the moon represent the ups and downs of the Christian life, which, Lesher implies, is not the model for a steady and strong reflection.

God's work on the fifth day consisted of creating the sea animals and the birds of the air. Having earlier identified water with the old sinful nature, Lesher here considers the sea animals, "teeming" in number, as symbolic of carnal passions, and animal lusts.

God's first act on the sixth day was to create cattle, creeping things, and wild animals. The three creations are a manifestation of the miracle of God's triune nature.

Humans were the crown of creation. Nothing was harmful to them so long as they remained faithful to God, but they failed to do this. (Lesher then moves rapidly through the fall, Christ's work, the reality of redemption, and the possibility of perfection.)

Persons in whom the full image of God has been restored can rule over the creature spirits. They can rule over the fish of the sea (carnal passions such as extravagant living, fancy dressing, and a wealthy lifestyle), over the birds of the air (arrogant and proudful people who oppress and control other people under the direction of the devil), and over animals (they rule over the animal by not loving the material things of the world, but by loving God with the "whole heart, the whole soul . . . and loving fellow humans as we love ourselves" [Luke 10:27]).

Lesher ends the chapter by indicating how the earth, given perfect creation, can be fruitful, such fruit in humans being spiritual and moral qualities. Thus flourishing plants could bring forth "sweet smelling spices, . . . useful for the honor of God, such as humility, lowliness and self-control, . . . and fruitful trees . . . bear . . . nourishing fruits, such as love, joy, peace, patience, friendliness, goodness, faith, gentleness, and chastity" (Gal. 5:22).

In this chapter, Lesher continues his symbolic and allegorical interpretation of Scripture. He uses this means to show the need for a sharp separation between God's and Satan's views of reality. Such separation stands over against the tendency in human civilization to incorporate all aspects of reality into one unified whole. This tendency is built on human perceptions and insights that are directly contrary to God's wisdom.

Lesher continues to emphasize gradual growth in spirituality and morality. Growth is the result of God's grace, self-denial, and total surrender. The goal of a "full and complete entry into God" can be realized.

Seven O'clock

Lesher begins this chapter by noting that because the number seven is mentioned so frequently in the Bible (especially in Revelation), God must have some special, or secret, meaning in the number. Although he disowns that the full meaning of the number has been revealed to him, he believes that some part of the meaning has been unlocked to his understanding. Accordingly, he wants "stutterling" to share his insights.

He outlines the seven spirits resting on Jesus (and to a lesser degree on Jesus' followers) and contrasts these with the seven spirits of Lucifer (the task of the seven evil spirits is to thwart the seven good spirits). He takes the number and basic idea of the spirits resting on Jesus from Isaiah 11:1-2 and Revelation 3:1, 5:6, and the seven spirits of Lucifer from Revelation 12:3. (The Berleburg Bible commentary on Revelation 12:3 lists seven evil spirits but the nature of these spirits is different from the characterization that Lesher gives them.)[14]

The first spirit resting on Jesus is the Spirit of the Lord, the pure Light. Those who follow Jesus will partake of that light. In contrast, the first spirit of Lucifer seeks to keep people in darkness and living unholy lives. If that effort fails, he becomes as an angel of light (Luke 16:8), telling people that there is no need for change; all that is needed is to pray and to go through the external forms of worship.

Wisdom is the second spirit with Christ and his followers. As Jesus grew in wisdom, stature, and favor with God and man (Luke 2:52), so his disciples are to mature in wisdom, humility, and the practice of the fruits of the Spirit. The second spirit of Lucifer, in contrast, works to keep believers in ignorance to prevent them from looking to God for wisdom.

The third spirit, understanding, rests on Jesus and is shared with his followers. This spirit consists of balanced spiritual and moral judgements and decisions (what to do and not to do), carried out in order and moderation. In contrast, the third spirit of Lucifer works to keep people in ignorance and blindness, making them satisfied with man-made forms of worship, accepting false teaching, and seeking human esteem and prestige.

The fourth spirit, the spirit of counsel, informed by the Counselor, leads people away from carnality and human prestige. It informs people what to do and gives them the power to do it. Lucifer's spirit endeavors to keep people satisfied with their old-nature way of living; if that is not successful, Satan tries to deceive them with earthly and untested counsel. This spirit may also direct people to listen to those who always talk of peace when they have never experienced true inner peace.

Another spirit resting on Jesus and his followers is power. Experienced through God's grace, this is the power of faith and courage, enabling believers to be strong, steadfast, and upright in love, no longer driven about by every new fad of false doctrine and no longer taken in by human craftiness. Lucifer's spirit is to keep the believer in a state of lethargy, created by the half truth that Christians are helpless creatures, unable to do anything without God working in them. After all, they say, God is merciful and will not hold us "so preciously accountable," because we are saved by faith, not by works. Such reasoning is "the language of the old serpent." Those holding such ideas will never enter into true repentance.

Confession is the sixth spirit, wherewith Christians are given inner assurance that they are children of God and fellow heirs with Christ. God's people have a heart knowledge of their oneness with the Father and the Son. The spirit of Satan tries to instill the idea that one cannot know if one is saved; the best one can do is to be rationally optimistic, trusting in the goodness of God.

The seventh spirit that rests on Jesus and is shared by his followers is the fear of the Lord. Although God's love has been poured into our hearts, Christians still have need to fear standing before God and his judgment; they should fear hell and damnation, fear offending God, and fear the "seventh, last, and greatest Antichrist." Satan's spirit, in contrast, is "the most dangerous and destructive of all for he is the last and greatest, the opposer of Christ" (2 Thess. 2; Rev. 13:11).

Lesher describes false understandings perpetuated by the evil, or strange, spirits. Some false spirits teach that in baptism the forgiveness of sins and the new birth takes place, and, relatedly, that baptism is the first step in being saved.

Lesher does not indicate what groups he had in mind, but his comment on baptism being the first step toward conversion probably was directed to those churches that practiced infant baptism. He very likely had the German Baptist Brethren in mind in his reference to forgiveness of sins and the new birth taking place at baptism. The Brethren in Christ believed that a heart-felt, new-birth experience, including the assurance of salvation given by the Holy Spirit, preceded water baptism.[15]

The German Baptist Brethren did not draw a sharp distinction between baptism and the new birth.[16] Alexander Mack, Sr., believed that baptism was a part of the process of conversion; his son, Mack, Jr., wrote that the reception of the Holy Spirit could precede or follow baptism.[17] In the first part of the nineteenth century, the German Baptist Brethren rejected the distinction made by the Brethren in Christ.[18] In 1815, they officially stated the position they rejected: "They require of a man, before he is to be baptized, that he should have passed entirely through repentance, and should have a lively experience of the forgiveness of sins, and that he should have obtained the new birth completely before baptism, so that they must confess such and be enabled to say how they came to it; and that only then they were fit to be received into the covenant."[19]

In other statements, the German Baptist Brethren declared that they found no such doctrine (or example) of the new birth completed before baptism: all that the gospel commanded was repentance, faith, and fruits in keeping with repentance (one of the fruits being baptism).[20] Dale Stoffer has summarized the German Baptist Brethren understanding of baptism during the nineteenth century as follows: "Without doubt, the predominant argument for the observance of baptism during this century is that it is connected with repentance and faith as a unit to which God has promised the remission of sins and the gift of the Holy Spirit. Thus God has ordained baptism as one of the means for the attainment of salvation. Not only is baptism commanded by God, it is also essential for salvation."[21]

Lesher ends this part of his discussion on baptism by affirming that the new birth is completed before baptism, and indicates that this has been his experience and that of many other Christians.[22]

He next champions the trine (three times) immersion mode of baptism. The first reference in the New Testament to baptism was John's baptizing of Jesus. "Mark it well!" Lesher writes. "It was not in a house but in the water" (Mark 1:9). It was in a place of much water so that immersion was possible. Also Philip took the eunuch in and out of the water. Futhermore, the apostles identified baptism as a burial (Rom. 6:4; Col. 2:12); burial means that a person is fully covered.

Lesher points to the early church father Tertullian who stated that the mode of baptism after proper spiritual preparation was trine immersion. Drawing from the *Martyrs' Mirror*, he adds that as of A.D. 620, there were those who practiced immersion baptism, and that in eastern and southern countries of Europe, the Greek words *baptisma* (baptism) and *baptizo* (to baptized) were understood to mean immersion. He uses material from Buck's *Theological Dictionary* to show that in the Greek Orthodox Church, the mode of baptism to the present day is immersion. The method of pouring was first introduced for sick persons, and not until the thirteenth century did pouring become the mode in the East.

The evil spirits, Lesher claims, brought about the pouring mode, the practice of baptizing innocent children, and the belief that the mode of baptism is of little importance. He calls on people's conscience to decide who is practicing baptism according to the Word of God and the model given by Jesus and his apostles.

He believes also that the evil or strange spirits brought the distortions practiced by some Christians in the Lord's Supper and feetwashing. (He gives fuller coverage to this subject in a later chapter.)

The false spirits have likewise distorted proper ideas about pride and dress. The Lord clearly taught and exemplified cross-bearing, self-denial, and a gentle and meek spirit. But many deceitful ministers, styling themselves as "preachers of justice," find the practice of humility and self-denial to be very difficult, thus they proclaim that style of dress does not matter. An excellent example of such a person is the rich man who dressed in costly garments, lived in a costly manner, and engaged in "excessive eating and drinking," but was not concerned about the condition of Lazarus. In both Testaments, pride and gaudy clothing are condemned (Jer. 3:18-24; 1 Tim. 2:8-10; Pet. 3:3, 5:5; James 4:6).

Lesher now turns his attention to defining the antichrist. He has no special revelation, he admits, about the Evil One other than the standard of truth—the Word of God.

Pointing to the biblical passage that prophesies that at the coming of the antichrist the works of Satan will be accompanied by signs and wonders and all kinds of deceptions, Lesher counters that true believers will be able to sort out most of the lies and test them by the truth. Those who seek God's will and are steadfast in his doctrine will know the truth which will make them free of error (John 7:17; 8:31,32).

Lesher, however, notes the need for discernment. Someone may be an able orator, a worker of miracles, a preacher of the biblical gospel of redemption who lives after the example of Christ, yet still can not be trusted for he can do such things working for Satan (Rev. 13:13,14; 2 Thess. 2:9). This has led some people to think that the antichrist will be born of an ungodly and corrupt virgin—a fake Christ.

Lesher summarizes the views of three people from the medieval world who held views on this subject. The first, Rabanus Maurus (776-856), about whom Lesher gains his information from the Berleburg Bible (Vol. 6, p. 734), believed that the antichrist will have a normal conception, but upon conception Satan will enter the mother. This will result in the child becoming the "height of wickedness and evil," and being known as the "Son of Corruption." Born in Babylon, he will set up his throne in Jerusalem, where he will kill the Christians he can not convert, rebuild the temple, have himself circumcised, announce himself as the Son of God, send preachers into the world, and perform many miracles, such as calling down fire from heaven. He will use a three-fold attack on Christians—terror, bribes, and miracles.[23]

Saint Bridget of Sweden (ca. 1303-1373), mystic and founder of the Order of Bridgettines, held views similar to those of Rabanus. Her most significant new idea was that the devil, out of jealousy, will try to destroy all of creation, just as God sought to save the world through one man. That man, terrible and horrible, born of an "accursed human," will be allowed by God to create the devil's empire and completely fulfill the prophecies of Revelation, chapter 13.[24]

Lesher also refers to the German abbess Hildegard (1098-1179), whom he characterized as "holy or saintly." On the basis of many visions, she believed that the mother of the antichrist, herself a practitioner of demonic arts, will teach her son, the Son of Perdition, those same arts. Possessed of those arts, he will perform many miracles, from calling down fire from heaven to raising the dead. His power will be shown by lightning, thunder, and hail. He will proclaim doctrines contrary to evangelical teaching, mocking humility, glorifying vanity and arrogance. Many believers will be swayed by him. To attract Jews he will reinstate circumcision and denounce baptism, the gospel, ordinance, and Jesus Christ. He will pretend to have been crucified and risen from the dead, and will present himself as the Savior of the world. In a climatic effort, he will gather his followers to attack heaven, only to be struck by God with a bolt of lightning on the top of a mountain.[25]

In this chapter, Lesher shows the influence of number symbolism and mysticism. At the same time, he is orthodox in thought and practice. Much of his wording is colored by Pietism with Anabaptist accents in evidence. The focus on wisdom is in keeping with radical Pietism. Incorporating the views of three medieval mystics is understandable because medieval mysticism was one of the roots of Pietism. His sense of separation is illustrated in the contrasts he draws between human wisdom and divine wisdom. His critical remarks on the conversion-discipleship differences with the German Baptist Brethren were undoubtedly made in part because the two groups had much in common. Lesher's emphasis on obedience was strongly Anabaptist. Whereas the Pietists were concerned with an inner obedience, Anabaptists stressed outer obedience. Lesher insisted on both.[26]

Eight O'clock

In this chapter Lesher considers emotions and shows how being born again transforms the nature and expression of those emotions. He lists eight: love, hate, lust/desire, loathing/aversion, joy/sadness, fear, and hope. He relates both the positive and negative aspects and expressions of each emotion as they move a person to salvation, holy living, and eternal life.

Here again he criticizes those who have only a nominal and external Christianity. In contrast, he uses John Bunyan to illustrate those who know and practice heart-centered living.

Hope, the last emotion listed, may serve to illustrate Lesher's thought. "This hope is sanctified and made alive by the truly newborn children of God so that they can say with Apostle Peter, "Blessed be God and the Father of our Lord Jesus Christ, who in His great mercy has caused us to be born again, and has renewed in us a new hope through the resurrection from the dead of our Lord Jesus Christ to an eternal and spotless inheritance which is preserved for us in heaven" (1 Peter 1:3,4). "This faith," Lesher says, "will become a living faith, and the hope will become a living hope, and these bring with them the greatest of all goodness, namely hope, and this hope will not permit itself to be made ashamed, for the love of God is sprinkled abroad in our hearts through the Holy Spirit . . . (Rom. 5:5), therefore also these three virtues remain, that is, faith, hope, and love but the greatest is love. . . ."

In this chapter, Lesher adds little that is new to his understanding of spiritual realities. As already noted, Pietists were emotionally oriented, thus Lesher again evidences his affinity to Pietism.

Nine O'clock

Lesher uses this chapter to define the nine beatitudes. He refers to them as "nine elements of blessedness," and explains them as nine elements of salvation, beginning with repentance and ending with persecution.

First beatitude: Blessed are those who acknowledge their spiritual poverty, sensing their inability to break the hold of sin.

Second beatitude: Blessed are those who feel the emotional intensity of being lost.

Third beatitude: Blessed are those who become meek and humble when they see the [fleeting quality] of worldly pleasures and realize the need for forgiveness.

Fourth beatitude: Blessed are those who realize that only Jesus can save and who begin to feel Christ drawing them to salvation.

Fifth beatitude: Blessed are those who, sensing that they are being drawn to the Son and begin to partake of the nature and virtue of Christ, become more merciful in helping others.

Sixth beatitude: Blessed are those who in all earnestness and industry seek a new heart, and receive the same by way of the Holy Spirit in a joyful and happy experience. The result is assurance of salvation.

Seventh beatitude: Blessed are the peaceable ones who gain true inner assurance, who stand firm in Christ, anointed and sealed by the Holy Spirit.

Eighth beatitude: Blessed are those who, in fulfilling all righteousness, are ready for persecution, follow the example of Christ, deny self, and rightly enter into baptism, feetwashing, and communion.

Ninth beatitude: Blessed are those who are persecuted on false charges. Rejoice and be comforted for you will be repaid in heaven. Respond patiently.

In commenting on the eighth beatitude, Lesher indicates that there is no command to use lamb as meat in love feast meals. In this he appears to be refuting the views of the German Baptist Brethren who in earlier years used lamb, although permitting beef, for its symbolic value.

Lesher also takes exception to a group who maintained that feetwashing should precede the meal and communion. Earlier they had practiced otherwise, but "some highly educated man" joined the group and, "with a semblance of order," convinced the body that the feetwashing service should be held before the agape meal. Now their members "publicly promote" this pre-meal practice.

Lesher says that he has heard some from this group say that Luther's New Testament translation regarding the timing of feetwashing is wrong. In response, Lesher relates that he consulted some "highly educated" people who knew Hebrew, Greek, Latin, and other languages; they assured him that Luther's translation was correct, that feetwashing did take place after the supper. Lesher ends by saying that true discipleship requires right practice.

German Baptist history indicates that at the beginning of their movement they did wash feet after the meal. When, however, a New Testament translation by Johann Heinrich Reitz, Dutch translator and radical Pietist, was published, the German Baptists, in keeping with the new translation, changed the practice from post-meal to pre-meal.[27] There can be little doubt that Lesher was refuting the German Baptist timing of feetwashing.

Lesher ends this chapter with one of his poems, which in translation loses some of its vitality.

> The sufferings here according to God's mind are
> to point out that those who dedicate their souls
> to do the Master's work, for whom the suffering
> of this world may continually serve His purposes,
> so that we in lowliness of heart, and that in humility
> we may grow and flourish, so that for all time on this
> earth we may be obedient and faithful to the Friend
> of our soul and becoming more and more in his image.

In chapter nine, Lesher interprets the beatitudes in terms of his understanding of conversion and the beginnings of the holy life of discipleship. Although most of the content is not freshly minted, the chapter again reveals the depth of his sincerity and commitment, and his claim that the true heart condition and intention will result in fulfilling all righteousness.

Ten O'clock

Lesher relates the tenth hour to the parable of the ten virgins (Matt. 25:1-13). He points out that there are many different opinions concerning the parable's meaning, but he intends not to be influenced by any of them.

Basic to his exposition is his allegorical treatment of the lamps of the virgins. The *lamp* itself, external and visible to the eyes, represents the external exercise of worship, such as baptism and feetwashing. The *wick*, partly visible, "typifies the testimony that comes from the lips" (what comes out of a person), and the *flame* is the "zeal . . . enthusiasm . . . [and] active force" (resulting in good deeds) of those who want to be at the heavenly banquet. The *oil* stands for the first love poured into the heart by the Holy Spirit's indwelling good nature. The oil is most basic for it is the source for all power and light. The message of the parable is that the oil needs to be replenished. The essential distinction between the foolish and the wise virgins was the inner heart condition of the latter.

The five foolish virgins, he goes on to say, were not a part of the great mass of nominal Christians who only go through the outer forms of religion. In fact, they were genuinely converted; they became "spiritual virgins" cleansed by the blood of Christ. The oil of love had been poured into their hearts, as evidenced by their going to meet the bridegroom. Their problem was that their first love dimmed and finally disappeared. They were satisfied with their "one-time change conversion." They did not obey all of Christ's commands, did not deny and mortify the self. Their fatal mistake was to allow the original "sweet . . . feeling, . . . the sweet incense of faith, and the living hope" to become weak. The five virgins did not go "forward in the course of holiness up to the indwelling and uniting with God."

One danger for the foolish virgins is that they did not fully realize that their oil supply was coming to an end. Lesher spiritualized this thought by saying that a false spirit can tempt Christians to think that it isn't necessary to be totally committed to God's will. A second danger is that as Christians become "faint and feeble," the tempter comes along and tries to convince them that their conversion was a human idea and not acceptable to God. As a result, people will come to believe that they can do no more. By such reasoning, half, if not more, of new Christians become foolish virgins.

The five wise virgins also began with genuine conversion experiences, but then realized the need to refill their lamps. They prayed about their condition, and as they prayed they became aware of a much brighter, more profound light, that outshone their usual understanding, just as the sun dims the moons and the stars. From the fulness of Christ, the committed receive grace and more grace (John 1:16). Those following the Lamb no longer find pleasure in extravagant and showy externals. By God's grace they become "faithful, upright, obedient souls." As the fully dedicated are increasingly attracted to God, they will see with greater insight their "fallibility and humanity," and know the need for more purification and sanctification before they can be fully united with God.

A secret to replenishing the oil is "inner humble quietness," together with inward prayer to God for help. Those who exercise themselves in prayer and in external works are attentive to the more internal doctrine and leading of the Spirit; such people will receive strength and renewal (Isa. 40:31). In climatic words Lesher wrote: "Finally with time and experience the power of the person's own natural life will be depleted and mortified, so that there will follow finally a fuller development of ourselves, or so to say a fuller possession or entrance of Jesus Christ will follow, and Christ can fully indwell and occupy our hearts through faith (Eph. 3:17). And at this point it can be said of us . . . 'I am crucified with Christ, but I am alive, yet not I, but Christ living in me.'"

At midnight the bridegroom came and the wise virgins, having an ample supply of oil, turned up their lamps with great joy. They met him with rejoicing because it was for love of him that they had denied themselves and sought to be faithful, even though at times they were hindered by their humanity. But the keeper of the gate will overlook such weakness because nothing was done wilfully.

The foolish virgins were in great fright when their lamps went out. The wise virgins refused to share their oil with them because the day of grace was over. Given the prospects of people being shut out of the kingdom like these foolish virgins, Lesher calls on his readers to be watchful and to stand firm in the faith.

At the end of the chapter, Lesher makes two points that are somewhat postscript in nature. First, he states that all ten virgins were called but only the five wise virgins were chosen. In saying this, he returns to the last chapter of his earlier work, The Small Spiritual Magazine, where he defined the called and the chosen in opposition to Calvinistic doctrine. Second, reverting to the same source, he claims that the wise virgins will reign with Christ during the millennium and have special privilege over the foolish virgins, who apparently (Lesher is not entirely clear) will have a second chance after the millennium.

In chapter ten, Lesher makes a genuine new birth the starting point in the Christian experience, yet the strongest emphasis is on the holy life that should follow that experience. He defines holiness basically as a condition of the heart as compared with the daily walk of discipleship. In the context of the revivalism of his day, Lesher understandably accentuated the holy life because this was the unique element that set the Brethren in Christ apart from groups like the United Brethren who were very focused on the new birth. An important part of the holy life was the quietistic note that Lesher stressed.

After making the case for real holiness, he seems to give those who were only converted a second chance in the new millennium (as he did in *The Small Spiritual Magazine*). In this way Lesher can still relate to those who do not follow a holy life, as defined by him.

Eleven O'clock

The parable of the workers in the vineyard (Matt. 20:1-18) who were sent to work in the eleventh hour is the basis for Lesher's eleventh chapter. He begins by showing how the different times workers were employed have been linked by some people to six dispensations: first hour, from the fall to God confronting Adam; third hour, Adam to Noah; sixth hour, Noah to Abraham; ninth hour, Abraham to Moses; eleventh hour, Moses to Christ; twelfth hour, Christ to the end of the visible world. This interpretation, Lesher claims, was that of the early church fathers.

But Lesher rejects this interpretation. Instead, he sees the times workers were sent to the vineyard as representing periods, both physical and spiritual, in the life of the individual, as follows: first hour, childhood to about fourteen years; third hour, years of youth, fourteen to twenty-eight years; sixth hour, "green blooming years," twenty-eight to forty or forty-five years; ninth hour, fading of vigor to fifty-five or sixty years; eleventh hour, old age to seventy or eighty years.

Himself in the last of these hours, Lesher urges youth to turn to God while their minds, wills, and hearts are strong and incisive, not when they are old because that is a time "full of trouble." In a long passage, partially quoted below in which he comments on Ecclesiastes 12, he vividly describes some of these old-age problems (was he referring to some that he had?): "Before the sun and the light, the moon and the stars become dark, and clouds come up after the rain (that is to say, when the eyes become dark and cloudly so that one can no longer see clearly because the brain is filled with moisture so that eyes and the nose water and drip, as is so often the case in old age), at the time when the watchers in the house tremble (that is when the hands with which one fends off the evil are so feeble that they tremble, . . .), and the strong ones bend (this refers to the legs that . . . in old age . . . bend out of shape so that they can scarcely bear up under the weight), and the millers that are now so few idly stand by (this speaks of the teeth of which only a few are left, and these are so dull and loose and unstable that they are almost useless . . .) . . . and when the almond tree blooms (that is when the hair on the head turns gray, and blooms like grave flowers) . . . before the silver cord is untied or comes away, and the gold fountain-head stops running or flowing and the bucket or bowl be broken at the well, or the wheel that brings up the water at the cistern be broken (the silver cord is the large pulse artery which carries the blood out of the heart and delivers the blood through smaller arteries to all parts of the body to every member, and through all the small vessels that lie close to the skin and back again to the heart, which makes up the circulatory system of the body, which is what Solomon here calls the wheel, which in old age begins to diminish its activity and become weaker, and the golden wellspring of the heart's blood begins to. diminish, ...)"

Having colorfully depicted the physical ailments of old age, Lesher emphasizes the value of the eternal soul in contrast to the mortal body. Body pleasures are poor enjoyment and transient because the body returns to the soil. Solomon was right when he wrote that all was vanity.

Returning to the parable, Lesher writes that the kingdom of heaven is like a landowner hiring people to work in his vineyard. The owner and the first workers agreed that the latter should work for a penny a day. The penny was given as to children, just converted, therefore still somewhat selfish and not ready to answer the call without receiving a reward. The penny was the "puniest form of salvation," only the first step of repentance. If the converted remain on this level, in the end they will receive only a penny. Only those who are faithful can come to a higher level of salvation and a greater degree of sainthood.

In sharp contrast, Judas turned away from his calling (he was both unfaithful and loved the rewards of unrighteousness). By his actions, he lost his penny, that is "the first degree of salvation." His actions were rooted in his free will and were not determined by unconditional election.

In considering the youth called in the third hour, Lesher is pleased that there are young people standing idle in the market place, because this means that they are not following the world in its "destructive activity." They heard God's call and responded, not even asking about their wages.

Passing over those hired in the sixth and ninth hours (as does the biblical account), Lesher asks why those hired in the eleventh hour were not hired earlier. Because some argue that they were idle because it was not yet God's time, Lesher embarks on another refutation of predestination, although he adds nothing essentially new to his argument. He emphasizes God's provision of salvation for all, God's "many devices and means to awaken people," the human responsibility of allowing God to awaken the sinner, and Satan's clever use of predestination as a discouraging element.

Lesher answers the question about why the last workers were not called earlier: they were too involved in the "rush and hurry . . . the lust and love" of this world. Only when, late in life, they had more time did they come to a halt and hear God's call.

In the evening, the workers were called and each paid a penny. Thus in the evening—at the time of death—each person will be shown whether they will receive either eternal rest or unrest. Later in the evening (at the end of the visible world), all will receive their wages, according to their works (Matt. 16:27).

When the early workers received the same wages as all the other workers, they complained of the owner's lack of justice. What is at issue, Lesher explains, is not the length of time served but the quality or depth of commitment. The goal is not selfish reward, rather it is a totally unselfish giving of one's self out of an unpretended love for Jesus, with the knowledge that salvation is due to the undeserved grace and mercy of God. Committed Christians faithfully follow Jesus with "all industriousness" to make their election sure. They seek through the power of God to further their purification and sanctification to experience the righteousness which is a fruit of God. Such Christians are sad that their human weaknesses keep them from honoring God more fully, but are joyful when they can do something for God.

Lesher ends the chapter by reaffirming that when people are saved by grace, they are to be received into the visible church of Jesus Christ, that church being the "community of the first-born whose names are written in heaven" (Eph. 2:19-22; 1 Pet. 2:5; Heb. 3:6,12).

Again in this chapter, Lesher continues to develop his basic ideas. In considering the meaning of the hours, he focuses on individual spirituality. His emphasis is on the holy life—a life divorced from the thoughts and practices of the world. The Christian must totally concentrate on being a faithful follower of God.

Twelve O'clock

In this chapter, Lesher returns to the subject of the end of history and the beginning of eternity. He also deals with this subject, as has been seen, in the last chapter of *The Small Spiritual Magazine*. Here, however, he does not consider the millennium; rather he is interested in the mission of the twelve apostles and the design of heaven.

Lesher claims that the number twelve, so often used in the Bible, especially in Revelation, "has great and wonderful mysteries of wisdom concealed in it." (He acknowledges that he has no special revelation regarding the mysteries.)

He first notes the twelve sons of Jacob, who were the basis for the twelve tribes of Israel, a people for whom God had "a very special calling." It appears (although the text is not clear) that Lesher related the special calling to the high priest's breast plate with the names of the twelve tribes on it, each tribe being represented by a precious stone (Exod. 28:17-21; 39:10-11).

He next suggests that all humanity can be divided into twelve groupings or classifications, not by genealogies or political nations, but according to their "innermost souls and dispositions," or their "creation features." Lesher bases this view on Deuteronomy 32:8 where when God determined the inheritance of the nations (sons of Adam), he separated them into the number of the tribes of Israel. Lesher's second authority for his position is the second-century church writing *The Shepherd of Hermas*. In this work, widely read in the second century and included in the Berleburg Bible, Herman is shown twelve mountains which "signify the twelve apostles within the entire circle of the earth."[28]

The significance of the twelve groups, Lesher proposes, is that each of the twelve apostles chosen by Christ had distinctive features and traits, special gifts and virtues. Thus when the twelve apostles were sent out into the world to spread the gospel, they were uniquely fitted, each apostle having the characteristics of one of the twelve groups. What Lesher has sketched here is a strategy for world-wide missions.

On the basis of Ephesians 2:19-22 and Hebrews 12:22-24, Lesher ties the evangelism of the apostles to the church and the eternal kingdom.

NOTES

[1]The full title in German (with original capitalization) is "Geistliche Uhrenerck als ein Zeugnisz der Wahrheit; besteht in zwelf Betrachtungen von eins bis zwelf uhr auf jede Stunde eine Betrachtung auf gesetzt und beschrieben." The full English title is, "The Spiritual Clockwork, as a Witness of the Truth Which Consists of Twelve Discussions from One to Twelve O'clock, for Each Hour One Discussion." Noah G. Good is a Pennsylvania-German scholar. I am working with the Good translation, edited by E. Morris Sider. The edited copy, Good's translation copy, and a photograph of the original document are all in the Historical Library and Archives at Messiah College.

[2]Personal interview with Peter C. Erb, September 23, 1989.

[3]Statements are drawn from John Joseph Stoudt, *Pennsylvania Folk-Art* (Allentown, Pa.: Schlechter's, 1948), p. 231, and from Andreas Bauer's fraktur booklet, 1833 (n.p.). The original document is in the Schwenkfelder Library, Pennsburg, Pennsylvania.

[4]John J. Davis, *Biblical Numerology* (Winona Lake, Ind.: BMH Books, 1968), pp. 103-156; Vincent Happer, *Medieval Number Symbolism* (New York: Columbia University, 1938), pp. 12-116; Isidore Kozminsky, *Numbers: Their Meaning and Magic*, ed. and rev. (New York: G.P. Putnam's, 1927), pp. 4-125.

[5]*A Companion to the Bible*, s.v. "Numbers," by J.J. von Allmen.

[6]Davis, *Biblical Numerology*, p. 146. Assigning numbers to letters, then dealing with the numbers to find mystical meaning was used to interpret Scripture in later Judaism and adopted by some early Christians. This system is known as Gematria. See *The International Standard Bible Encyclopedia*, s.v. "Number," by B.C. Birch, and *The Encyclopedia of Religion*, s.v., "Numbers," by Anne Marie Schimmel.

[7]Stoffer, *Brethren Doctrines*, p. 19.

[8]Kozminsky, *Numbers*, pp. 123-124.

[9]Lesher, *Spiritual Clockwork*, p. 4.

[10]Rufus M. Jones, *Spiritual Reformers in the 16th and 17th Centuries* (Boston: Beacon Hill Press, 1959), pp. 158-164.

[11]Happer, *Medieval Number Symbolism*, p. 35. Some of the early church fathers, beginning with Irenaeus, identified the four living creatures with the four Gospels: Matthew (human-faced man), Mark (lion), Luke (calf), John (Eagle). William Barclay, *The Revelation of John*, Vol. 1 (Philadelphia: The Westminster Press, 1960), pp. 202-203.

[12]Peter C. Erb to author, August 28, 1989, and interview with Erb.

[13]Interview with Erb.

[14]This difference in usage helps to confirm the basic impression that Lesher consulted the Berleburg Bible but was not a devotee of it.

[15]Schrag, "Attitude to the World," p. 31.

[16]Alderfer, "The Mind of the Brethren in Christ," p. 76; Wittlinger, *Quest for Piety and Obedience*, p. 63.

[17]Stoffer, *Brethren Doctrines*, pp. 76, 95.

[18]*Minutes of the Annual Meetings*, pp. 49-51, 56-57, 185-186.

[19]Ibid., pp. 50-51.

[20]Donald F. Durnbaugh, "Nineteenth-Century Dunker Views of the River Brethren," *Mennonite Quarterly Review* (April 1993), 133-151.

[21]Stoffer, *Brethren Doctrines*, p. 109.

[22]Both groups believed in fulfilling all righteousness (Matt. 3:15), and were strongly committed to Anabaptist discipleship. But between the founding of the German Baptist Brethren and the beginning of the Brethren in Christ, a stronger emphasis on the crisis conversion experience developed in Pietism.

[23]Rabanus Maurus was Archbishop of Mainz. He is best known for his views of the Roman Catholic interpretation of the Eucharist. *New International Dictionary of the Christian Church*, s.v. "Rabanus Maurus," by C.G. Thorne, Jr.

[24]*Dictionary of Church History*, s.v. "Bridget of Sweden," by J.D. Douglas.

[25]Ibid., s.v. "Hildegard," by Robert C. Clouse.

²⁶For background on the assessments in the paragraph, see the following sources: Chauncy David Ensign, "Radical German Pietism" (Ph.D. diss., Boston University, 1955), p. 330; Stoeffler, *Evangelical Pietism*, pp. 9-23, 15-16, 80-87; Stoffer, *Brethren Doctrines*, pp. 83-84; Peter C. Erb, *Pietists, Protestants, and Mysticism* (Metuchen, N.J.: Scarecrow Press, 1989), pp. 156-191.

²⁷Donald F. Durnbaugh, ed., *The Brethren in Colonial America* (Elgin, Ill.: The Brethren Press, 1967), p. 464; *Brethren Encyclopedia*, s.v. "Love Feast," by Graydon F. Snyder; Stoffer, *Brethren Doctrines*, p. 91.

²⁸The *Shepherd of Hermas* was the most popular of all the non-canonical books of the New Testament. It is found in some of the earliest Bibles, such as Sinaitcus and Bezae. It was quoted as inspired Scripture by such early church fathers as Irenaeus and Origen. The church historian Eusebius stated that it was publicly read in the churches and thought to be "necessary for those who have need of elementary instruction." Lesher accepted the belief that the author of the *Shepherd of Hermas* was the Hermas mentioned in Romans 16:14. These views are not accepted by modern scholars. See Norman L. Geisler and William E. Nix, *A General Introduction to the Bible* (Chicago: Moody Press, 1968), p. 203.

Donors

The following people donated funds for the publication of this book.

L. Bedsaul and Verda M. Agee
George M. and Lois K. Beck
Terry L. and Debra Brensinger
Michael R. and Lena H. Brown
A. Graybill and Ethel S. Brubaker
Merle and Ida J. Brubaker
Ruth A. Brubaker
Samuel M. and Lucy Brubaker
Wade G. and Linda A. Burkholder
John A. and Esther B. Byers
D. Wayne and Ruth A. Cassel
Leonard and Ruth Ann Chester
Daryl and Lois Climenhaga
Arthur M. and Lona S. Climenhaga
Steven and Marlene Lesher College
Eber B. and Ruth M. Dourte
Lois Lesher Eberly
Eastern Mennonite Associated
    Libraries and Archives
Noel Falk
William and Maxine Lesher
    Gindesperger
Dorothy Jean Gish
Ethan M. and Elizabeth A. Gramm
Shirley Groff
Robert E. and Judith C. Hamilton
Isaiah B. and Doris B. Harley
D. Ray and Susanne E. Heisey
J. Wilmer and Velma I. Heisey
Russell S. and Linda M. Hepler
Sara E. Herr
Robert A. and Anna Mary Hess
William R. and Nancy J. Hoke
Kenneth B. and Erma L. Hoover
Paul E. and Lela M. Hostetler
D. Ray and Audrey F. Hostetter
Luke L. and Doris L. Keefer
George P. and Kathleen K. Kimber
H. Frank and Lois A. Kipe
Homer L. and Mildred L. Kraybill

Howard L. and Ruth E. Landis
Samuel Lenhert
Edith M. Lesher
Emerson L. and Ruth D. Lesher
James J. and Margaret A. Lesher
J. Ira and Naomi R. Lesher
Marvin M. and Mary G. Lesher
Willis and Evelyn Lesher
Alden M. and Mary K. Long
David P. and Lois McBeth
Donald E. and Verna E. (Lesher)
    Martin
Anna Verle Miller
Ronald L. and Joyce H. Miller
Robert J. and Marian L. Musser
Benjamin W. and Lorraine S. Myers
Paul W. and Laura Nisly
Karl M. and Connie Oberholser
C. Jack and Rebecca K. Orr
Clyde A. and Marilyn L. Ross
Kevin and Gail Ryan
E. Morris and D. Leone Sider
Robert D. and Lura Mae Sider
Roger C. and Joanne Sider
Ronald J. and Arbutus Sider
Ronald R. and Beth F. Sider
Elbert N. and Arlene J. Smith
James and Deborah Sollenberger
R. Sheldon and Marie E. Starr
Richard A. and Pauline E. Stevick
John K. and Jane H. Stoner
Erla Z. Stump
LeRoy and Sue Walters
Donna F. and Carlin Wenger
L. Eugene and Darlene R. Wingert
Paul E. and Gertrude M. Witter
Eric and Emily Lesher Wolgemuth
John R. and Anna M. Yeatts
Lawrence M. and Shirlee K. Yoder
Ruth M. Zercher